2 Kids, A Taco, and Cancer

RUB SOME DIRT ON IT~YOU'LL BE FINE

Shawna Weber

Contributions from Zach Weber

DEDICATION

I am dedicating this book to my family. Zach, because he has been my rock and the voice of reason so often throughout this journey. Jack, because he has had to grow up fast for a 6-year-old and has had some life lessons I wish could have waited a while. He has a kind heart and unconditional love for his sister, even if they fight all the time. And, of course, Lucy. She is the reason this book even came to light. While I hate the circumstances, and I wish she never had to experience cancer, she has taught me so much and made me a better mother. She has taught me that life is about living now. Do what we love and do it with intention and passion. And last, but certainly not least, Taco. Taco has been our faithful wiener dog. He has endured being away from us during this time; he has dealt with Lucy putting clothes and make up on him and dressing him as a baby. He has cuddled me more times than I can count and let me cry deep into his brown face.

CONTENTS

ACKNOWLEDGMENTS

I want to thank my husband for encouraging me to finish writing this; if it weren't for his consistent nagging, I may not have even given it a thought. I also have to thank all the supporters who followed us through our journey. You have become family, and I love how you love my daughter. I never expected so much support and love for this blog or for Team Lucy. It was simply a way for me to cope with a horrible situation, and instead, you said my words were inspiring. Thank you for that. Thank you to St. Jude. I don't have any other words to describe the thanks I owe them. And of course all my A. L. L. mamas, cancer mamas, and onco moms. Thank you for your support, knowledge, and bookless book clubs. I love you all even thought I have yet to meet most of you in person. And I have to say thank you to wonderful friend who took time out of her life to edit this book for me. I'm sure it was no easy task as most of it was written with pure emotion with no regards to any format. Thank you, Anita.

Chapter 1
BC (BEFORE CANCER) & WHAT IS A BLOG BOOK?

Before December 26, 2010, our family was your typical American family with 2 kids, a dog, and 2 cars. Zach and I both worked in the corporate world. Jack had just started Kindergarten, and Lucy went to a daycare. We were very busy as most young families are. The week was consumed with work, errands, and running a household, while the weekends were treasured days to stay home and relax and spend time with our kids. I think we saw each other for about 2-3 hours each day during the week, so we saved the weekends for all the fun stuff. We loved to be spontaneous and take the kids for a trip over the weekend. We also liked to send the kids to grandma's once a month to have some time ourselves. Managing a household and working at a marriage wasn't easy. We were just starting to pass down traditions to the kids, and they were beginning to cherish them. They had just turned 5 and 3, so they were able to understand the importance of creating our own family rules. We were out of the baby stage, we had both worked our way up in our careers, so we were starting to live comfortably and no longer paycheck to paycheck, with the help of Dave Ramsey. We were evolving like most young families do. Our priorities were different before that day. Our dreams were the same, but put back on a much higher shelf. Then December 26, 2010 changed our life as we knew it, and we would never go back to our "normal" again.

Before I continue with this book, I need to explain a few things. This book is one in a series of three online journals I kept while we have watched our daughter battle leukemia. I have decided not to change anything that was written or add any new insights that I have now, that I may not have had when I first wrote the entries. These are all my thoughts, interpretations, and opinions about our treatment and the life we were living at the time. Some things, you will find, change as I learn more. Also, there must be an understanding that this was, and still is, my therapy, so most entries were written with raw emotion. I chose not to change that portion nor add any explanations or hind sights to my entries. You will find this book to be quite different from any other in that its always in first person, and always in a conversational tone. You must imagine yourself sitting across from me and having a cup of coffee. Or sometimes wine. Lots of wine. I, in no way, represent St. Jude and all opinions in this book are of my own gathering.

If this is the first time you have read this, I suggest a box of tissues, and be prepared to cry and laugh. If you have followed me on this journey and read all my blog entries, I must warn you that going back and reading the beginning was very hard for me. It may be for you too.

Each entry is date and time stamped at the exact time I posted the entry on Caringbridge. I have also inserted the number of days we are into treatment to help give you a better idea of how much has happened in such a short period of time.

Our day of diagnosis came on December 26, 2010. I start my journal on day 2, December 28, 2010.

amazon.com

**www.amazon.com/
your-account**

For detailed information about this and
other orders, please visit Your Account.
You can also print invoices, change your
e-mail address and payment settings,
alter your communication preferences,
and much more - 24 hours a day - at
http://www.amazon.com/your-account.

	Item Price	Total
	$14.99	$14.99
		$14.99
		$14.99
it		$14.99
		$0.00

ıg.

Returns Are Easy!

Most items can be refunded, exchanged,
or replaced when returned in original
and unopened condition. Visit http://
www.amazon.com/returns to start your
return, or http://www.amazon.com/help
for more information on return policies.

Gift Cards
Millions of items. No expiration.
www.amazon.com/giftcards

amazon.com

Your order of August 30, 2012 (Order ID 103-3147963-131380⁴

Qty.	Item
1	**2 Kids, A Taco, and Cancer: Rub Some Dirt in IT ~ You'll be Fine (Volume 1** Weber, Shawna M --- Paperback **(** P-1-Q38C44 **) 0988207400**

Subtotal
Order Total
Paid via cre
Balance du

This shipment completes your order.

Have feedback on how we packaged your order? Tell us at www.amazon.com/p

CHAPTER 2
OUR INTRODUCTION TO LEUKEMIA AND ST. JUDE
CHILDREN'S RESEARCH HOSPITAL

Day 2, Dec 28, 2010 10:46pm
Today was the longest, and yet most satisfying, day we have had so far. Waiting and not knowing has been the worst. We now know what Lucy has for sure, her treatment plan, and are slowly accepting the fact that the "c" word is a part of our lives and Lucy's forever. We try to say it as often as possible, and let Lucy and Jack know that her blood is very sick with cancer bugs. I'm not sure how she feels or what her little three year old mind is thinking.

I *can* say St. Jude is wonderful. We found out we have the BEST doctors in the WORLD! People fight for these doctors, and we are fortunate to have landed with them. And of course, once anybody sees that little Beatle-loving girl, they fall in love with her like we did the moment we met her. She has a feisty spirit, and we are certain if she knew what "flipping the bird" meant, she would be doing that to her cancer.

I cannot believe how our lives have changed in a matter of days. Today, she received three surgeries at once. She had a miniport inserted above her heart to help give her chemotherapy and do blood draws so she doesn't have to get "stuck" all the time, she had a spinal tap done to see how many cancer cells are living in her spinal fluid and near her brain, and a bone marrow sample to see the same for what is living in her bones. Good news: so far no cancer cells in her spinal fluid or near her brain. But her bone marrow is saturated. Doc says that is normal, which is why she has already had one treatment of chemo injected in her spine and is having another put in her IV as I type. What a brave little girl. All of this and she still managed to eat her food like she was inhaling it and yell at the nurses when they were taking her vitals. She said, "I am sleeping, leave me alone!" Little booger. Of course, they love her more for that.

We also got our temporary housing set up today. We are going to take turns sleeping in a real bed and trying to be "normal" every other day. Our new normal is something that doesn't take long to adjust to when your child has leukemia

Day 4, Dec 29, 2010 1:05pm
Today has been a slower paced day, but it is almost more emotional and scary than the previous days because we are able to absorb information, educate ourselves, and realize how wonderful St Jude is and how fortunate we are to be here out of all places in the world.

I'm learning all about chemotherapy, but not very fast. She has so many different types on different days. Some are given through IV, others are given through her spinal tap, and some are given through her mouth.

Some are super-strong, so much so that if we have to help her go potty, we must wear gloves because it secretes through the urine. Poor tiny thing. I asked the doctor for a list of names and times in a reader friendly format, so I can try to figure it all out.

We did find out today that the spinal fluid is clear from cancer cells. They thought so yesterday, but wanted to double check and confirm. We also found out the genetic makeup of her cancer, and it is the "good" kind that doesn't normally come back, so that means that her chemotherapy will be a little less intense. Good and cancer in the same sentence...hmmm.

So here is how this works, and mind you, I'm still learning too. Leukemia is cancer of the blood, so basically her entire tiny body, from her toenails to her hair, is infected. It is a fast and furious cancer that multiplies by thousands in a short time. BUT, that is better than a slow-growing cancer because it responds to chemotherapy much better. So basically, during the first two weeks, which is called Induction, she will get so much chemotherapy that it will kill every cancer cell in her body and kill some of the good ones too. So much so that it will kill her entire immune system.

So the first 30 days are important for two reasons: 1st it kills all the cancer cells and 2nd because she will be so vulnerable to ANY type of infection from colds, flues, and even foods that may harbor bacteria. Anything in her room that has sat for an hour must be thrown away. She can't even have toys that can't be thoroughly washed each night, and we have to wash blankets and clothes every night too. She can't have anything from back home because any type of bacteria or virus can be harbored in it(that's why I said no packages until we are in the clear).

It will take her system approximately 2 weeks to get back to a count of 500 after it hits zero. She has to brush her teeth 4 times a day and we, of course, have to wash our hands no less than 15 times a day! Anytime we leave and anytime we enter her room, we wash them. It's a little scary to think that when we leave the hospital, we will be responsible for keeping infection away. It's also a horrible dilemma we have.

The first 30 days are the most critical, so neither of us wants to leave, but we have Jack at home. He can't come here because of the risk of infection, and if one of us went home and we take turns, we run the risk of bringing infection back. So this is our toughest dilemma. We still don't know what to do.

After the second phase of her chemo, we do another Reinduction phase to ensure that all the cancer cells are out of her body and not hiding. During this she will also get about 16-32 spinal taps with chemo to check, since that's where leukemia likes to hide. Then, if her tests come back good, she is fighting, and the cancer cells stay away, we will get to go home. We will still have to stay on the low bacteria diet in addition to a low salt and diabetic diet. The steroids she is on are part of her chemo, but they also can cause other side effects, thus the diet.

Day 4, Dec 29, 2010 10:20pm
So we are moving into the Ronald McDonald house tomorrow, and Lucy's doctor, Dr. Pui, says that she may get to come with us either Friday or Saturday to live with us! Yea! It's exciting, but scary too. Just one infection or cold could really put us back in

inpatient care, and possibly ICU. UGH!

Day by day, day by day. I keep telling myself that, but I don't do well with day by day. I'm a big picture thinker, and I like to plan. I am finding that is something that you can't really do with leukemia. I also have to say thank you to everybody. I truly believe everybody's well wishes, prayers, and positive thoughts have landed us where we are now.

Lucy is a part of a clinical study. So basically, they only take so many children for this type of treatment. There are families that come here and live and come every day to ask to be seen by St. Jude. They get turned down because the CDC only allows so many children in this study. Basically, the reason behind that is because she is getting way more chemo than the manufacturers recommend. The CDC and FDA won't approve the treatment she is getting at any other facility. And, if the study is full, the children have to go and get treated at a different facility that doesn't do the same "protocol" that St. Jude does. Protocol is treatment. Lucy's doctor is the best in his field. We had no idea. He is highly sought after, and I feel so privileged that he agreed to take Lucy. I honestly had no idea that it was an option NOT to take her.

When Peoria called down here, they could have said no, that they were full. It's like everything aligned at the right time. If I had waited one more day to take her to the doctor, we may have missed our opportunity to bring her here. And I know for a fact that everybody sending out their thoughts has helped us get this lucky.

Tomorrow is a new day; I have yet to look up what is on her schedule. It's so overwhelming, and I am just now learning how to pronounce all her drugs. I'm also seeing the side effects of chemo and steroids.

Her cheeks are so darn chubby and cute, but sad too. She won't poop. She tells everybody, "No thank you, I'll poop when I get home." So my goal for tomorrow: Get the girl to poop! Ha!

She is also getting agitated by the drugs, which is totally normal, but very stressful on Zach and me. You can't discipline a child on Prednisone. And you really don't want to discipline a child with cancer, so we just yell at each other. :)

Of course, everybody that knows us, also knows we have to be inappropriate about it as well. I mean she has cancer. There is nothing we can do about it but help the doctors with the protocol and be there to hold her hand and let her get all her frustrations out on us, so we have to get in a laugh or two, or we would go crazy. Lucy was crying and whining and I asked what was wrong, and Zach said "Oh, she thinks she should be spoiled because she has cancer." I mean really. That's funny stuff! Inappropriate, but funny. Plus, it helps to let Lucy see us still laugh and joke -- not sure what the nurses think of us yet! But, they love Lucy, so that's all that matters. They melt when they meet her. And who wouldn't? Right? Again, thank you for the support; you don't even know how comforting it is. People have asked about an address to send things to Lucy and right now we can't have any packages due to risk of infections and bacteria, but as soon as she can, I will post her address.

Day 5, Dec 30, 2010 8:41am
Ever seen 'The Exorcist'? When the girl sits up in her bed and her head spins? That's Lucy this morning. During her Prednisone spells, we call her Lucifer. Take the normal 3-year-old attitude and mix in a cocktail of meds, feeling like shit, not sleeping, and not having the words to explain how she is feeling, and you get this girl who I have no idea who she is.

They said it's going to get worse. Oh boy! She threw her puke bucket at me this morning and told me to get out of her room. I did. I promptly left and waited outside the door until she wanted me to come back in. So I can definitely say that today, I'm thankful for Xanax.

So update on her health: Her blood pressure spiked during the night, so they are giving her meds for that. Her ANC white blood count is down to 100. There are three cells in your white blood count, this is the one that fights infection. If it's under 500, you are at high risk for anything. But this is all part of the process. Her count will get all the way to zero, then slowly climb back up. She also has a bad cough today, so they are doing a chest X-ray to make sure pneumonia hasn't set in. Although, her tubes from her ears have fallen out, so they think it could be the fluid and congestion from that. Might get a new set of tubes if that's the case.

Biggest thing I learned through the night: I am her advocate. If I want something, I ask, and then I tell them. And it's usually done. Never had that at any other doctor. So it's scary, but comforting at the same time.

Day 5, Dec 30, 2010 10:16pm
Hour by hour, things change dramatically. Last night was rough for Lucy; her blood pressure was high and she kept getting headaches. Then this morning, Dr. Pui came in and requested his entire staff to come to the room as well. Talk about scaring the crap out of us. We had no idea why 6 doctors were huddled in her room. He was really agitated by the blood pressure. Apparently, if it gets too high, she can start having seizures. So they started her on two different types of meds to get it down. It did go down, but then she started to run a fever and she has a terrible cough, which is scary because we don't want her to have an infection now. They sent cultures off to see if it is, in fact, a bacterial infection and did a chest x-ray. We will know in 48 hours.

Then, Lucy seemed to perk up after she got some sleep, got the blood pressure down, and started antibiotics. We took a trip together in a wheelchair to get a CT scan of her bone density and chest x-ray. Holding her on my lap while we were going to the Chili's building broke my heart. She was so fragile and I didn't get much out of her for conversation. It really makes me sad and for that moment, I really saw how sick she was. It took some persuading to get her to do the x-ray, but she got to pick out some toys for being a big girl when she got pictures taken of her bones and chest. She wanted to show them to Jack. That was the first thing she said, and it broke my heart. She just held on to them tightly as we were wheeled back to the room.

When we got back to the room, she had to take her medicine, which is a horrible battle. One of the nurses explained it to me, and it makes sense. She has no control over anything right now. She is meeting a ton of different people, having all sorts of things done to her, she can't even sleep or poop without somebody examining it. And for a 3-year-old who is trying to be independent, this is big. So she refuses to take her medicine and go to the bathroom because it's the only thing that she can control.

Tonight, I let her do her own medicine. Then the poor baby threw it all up. So we have to do it again in an hour. They gave her anti-nausea meds and after they settle in, we shall try again. Her blood pressure is still also very high. They are doing another med and IV meds. And she started developing a rash on her back. Going to be a long night... .I don't even know what day/night it is.

Day 6, Dec 31, 2010 10:47am
Plan for the weekend: Keep Lucy's blood pressure under control and the fever away. They are trying a different mix of meds. They explained to us that it's really a matter of seeing how each individual reacts to the meds and finding the "right" dose for her. The fever has not returned since she has been on antibiotics. They also said so far day 1 of the blood culture shows no infection; they will continue to monitor it every day. But this is good news. Also her blood work looks good. The ANC white count is still at 100, so on day 7, she will receive the next dose of the strong chemo that should bring that count to zero. That SHOULD mean all the cancer cells are gone. But it's not always the case. Then as the count comes back up, it SHOULD be normal white blood cells. These are all best case scenarios, which is what I am shooting for. Amazing how they can pinpoint all these things and predict their behavior. They are like a living organism with a habitat. Amazing how much research has been done and how far they have come. Lucy probably won't get to move in the Ronald McDonald House until Monday, which I am fine with. She won't go until her blood

pressure is under control.

How are mom and dad doing? Tired. We have only snapped at each other like 3 times, and that's better than at home, so I think we are good. We haven't broken down, and now it seems futile to do so. She is the one allowed to break down; she is doing all the work. She has cancer, and it is what it is. It sucks, but we aren't dwelling on the diagnosis; we are looking at recovery. We can't plan anything right now, so that's a little hard. I like to plan everything. I only get angry when she has a bad hour.

We are trying to stick to routine as much as possible. She has nap time with a ritual, bed time, etc. We are also starting to discipline again. No spankings, so don't worry! HA! The nurses say she will get better and, when she does, if we haven't stuck to "normalcy," we will have a monster on our hands. Daddy is much better with it, though. I'm a sucker and give in more often. Again, not so different from home :), but its hard seeing her in that hospital bed.

Well, Lucy is taking a nap and I will join her. Sleep when she sleeps, like when you have a new baby. Again, easier said than done.

Day 6, Dec 31, 2010 11:23pm
Today, Lucy was able to have much better blood pressure until this evening when it spiked again. She also had a low-grade fever. We were hoping to take her down to the 2nd floor where they have a juke box that has the Beatles on it and have a New Year's Eve party, but due to those things, we couldn't leave the room. So I found some balloons and brought the party to her. She loved them and made us wrap a balloon around each of her baby doll's hands.

She seems to be having all the side effects of Prednisone. Doc says some kids have some and others none. She has almost all of them. Today, she threw up quite a bit. I did ask for them to give her Benadryl so she could get some sleep. She's having a hard time with that. The doctors and nurses are amazed with her spirit and independence. When she doesn't feel good, we give her the mp3 player and she listens to the Beatles. It's her "zone". The doc said its awesome she can calm herself like that, and most adults cant. She is also getting used to all her wires and the IV cart. She is trying to establish a routine. She tells us, and the nurses, how to do things. I think it gives her more control and her attitude is slightly better. She does ask to go home often, but then again, so do I.

Zach made me come back to the bed and rest tonight. He says I need it, and he is right. I just feel an enormous amount of guilt when I leave her. But I guess if I get run down and sick, I'll be no good to her. So it's a hot bath and lots of sleep for me. I hope. Sleeping here is the hardest part. I get homesick. Tomorrow, I'm going to run to the store and get some food. The cafeteria food blows!

I think we have made up our minds about Jack. As soon as she gets through day 7 of her chemo, and we get her blood count, we will probably go pick him up to be here as long as he's not sick. Neither one of us can imagine leaving Lucy, nor being away from Jack. It'll be tight quarters, but hopefully better for all of us to be together. They say this first Induction is intense the first two weeks, then the next 5 weeks after that are a little better. The average family stays here for 7 weeks in the beginning. So we won't be home until at least then. Shooting for mid Feb. Here I go making plans again!! Can't help but look forward to when we can bring her home.

She got a dose of chemo called Peg (it's actually really long and scientific name), and it's pretty powerful. It's the main drug that makes her hair fall out. When she gets to come back to the RMH, we are going to let her cut her own hair. Give her some control over it, and they say it's easier on mom ;) because it will be easier to manage once it starts falling out in clumps. So we are going ultra-short!!! Perhaps mom and dad will go ultra-short too. ;) I think dad even plans on shaving his entire head. What a great daddy.

Well no more chemo till Tuesday, just Prednisone. But ironically, she's doing great with the chemo, and it's the Prednisone that tears her up.

Day 7, Jan 1, 2011 10:54am
They are giving Lucy Zofran before her meds now to help with the vomiting. They can only give it twice a day, so our 2 o'clock meds may still cause some problems. Blood pressure was slightly elevated this morning, but seems to be better. She actually felt like getting out of her room today for longer than 5 minutes! Yay! We listened to the Beatles on the juke box, then went to the toy room for 20 minutes. And she was mad when we had to leave to get her blood. Pui came in and said low salt and low bacteria diet now. So no more bacon; she will be disappointed! But, he said she's looking really good, and it looks like the chemo is working great already. They won't know for sure until day 15 and she gets another bone marrow aspiration. I'm thankful for the good hour we had. Now to the next hour.

Day 7, Jan 1, 2011 10:42 pm
Today was a great day for Lucy. She ate better, no throwing up, and slept pretty well considering all the nurses coming in and out to change her meds and take her BP. She and I also fought a lot today. Which means she was feeling good. That is totally normal! We have such similar personalities, we butt heads. Doc still wants to keep her until we can go a certain period without high BP. She did better today, and it was elevated just once. They also got cultures back from her blood and no bacterial infection. They stopped one antibiotic and will stop the other tomorrow. She is also on day 5 of her protocol and no chemo yesterday or today. She gets chemo again on day 7, so day 8 and 9 will be rough.

Zach says her hair is coming out easier already, so we will take lots of pictures tomorrow because when it grows back, it may grow back totally different. It can be thicker and curly. Can you imagine?? Her hair MORE thick?? It can also come in thinner, but most folks lean towards thick. She did get a bath today and got her hair washed. She enjoyed her 15 minute bubble bath.

She is adjusting ok. She is homesick. I hope when we come to the RMH all together and Jack gets here, that will be better. But, she's getting a routine. When we take her to the bathroom, she tells us to watch her wires (IV cords), and put on gloves, and watch her "buddy". Her med port is named "buddy" because it helps her not have to get poked all the time.

She has stopped talking to doctors! She also doesn't like when we are talking to anybody in her room about anything. She blames them! And they just love her. She is getting quite spoiled. And all she hears is how beautiful she is. Which, of course, is true!

The cancer no longer scares me. She will fight that and win. It will be hard and long, but she will prevail. It's the lifestyle and care we are going to have to ensure over the next three years. I mean no more BBQs, cook outs, no more food from anyone anywhere!! We have to give her certain foods and ensure when they were cooked. And then keep her away from bacterial infections. You know how hard that will be? Our house will have to be spotless beyond belief, and she can't go to daycare, so that puts a wrench in what we will do for work. Our nasty well water will have to be treated beyond imagination and that's just for bathing. Drinking water will be bottled from now on. No fresh fruits or vegetables unless it has a hard rind. No house plants. And probably no big gatherings without a mask and only for a short period of time. No tea or tea products at all. Can't be around cats and litter boxes. Oh and there is more. This is what scares me. The doctors are doing such great work and I may screw it up!! And we still have to live a "normal" life.

I told Zach it's like having a new baby all over again. When we brought Jack home, we were both so scared, and had no clue what to do... that's how I feel now. He is a champ though. He does better about not freaking out and telling me we will manage.

He's staying with Lucy again tonight because I about had a nervous breakdown when the nurse was telling me about how other kids died and what from. I about knocked her out. Thanks to him for being wonderful

Day 8, Jan 2, 2011 9:58am
Well, Lucy got some restless sleep last night. We are going to talk to the doctor about some sleeping medicine. She is a bear without the sleep. Plus Tuesday is strong chemo day; she will need all the rest she can get. She is getting tired of being in bed, and I can't blame her. Today, we find out if we get to go to the Ronald McDonald House. It will be either today or tomorrow. We still have to get "learned" on everything. And get hands on training, but I will definitely keep everybody posted. We are so nervous to go outpatient....

Day 8, Jan 2, 2011 11:37am
Tomorrow we move to RMH! Yay! We still come to the hospital every day for treatment, but only for a few hours, and at least we have a bed to sleep in.

Day 8, Jan 2, 2011 10:49pm
Lucy's ANC count is back up to 100 again, which is good. It is supposed to bottom out at zero and then slowly rise. The only problem: she gets chemo again Tuesday, so it will crash again. Now is the critical time for keeping her away from infection and even colds. She is so ready to go home. She doesn't sleep for crap here with somebody going in every hour to check on her. I asked for them to give her Benadryl tonight, she needs the rest.

So, the next 5-6 weeks are going to be a whirlwind and touch and go. We are going to aim for no hospital stays, but everyone said that its normal for us to have to come back to inpatient 2-3 times, maybe more. If she gets a fever or anything, she's in. Even though sometimes the cancer breaking out of her cells causes fevers, they don't want to risk it, and I'm thankful for that.

So every Tuesday, for the next 6 weeks will be rough chemo day. Wednesday and Thursday is also chemo, and every other day is blood draws. So we will be going back and forth from RMH to hospital. And then day 15 will be the day that tells us how the rest of our therapy is going to go. It's D-day in that we will know if the chemo is working or not. That decision will decide our lives for the next year. So it's pins and needles until then.

Day 9, Jan 3, 2011 11:07am
So we don't get to go to the RMH after all. Dr Pui wants to take Lucy off some meds and see how she does. It's a good thing to take her off all maintenance drugs since the chemo is poison enough for her little body.

Tomorrow is strong chemo day, so based on her reaction, we may or may not go outpatient. We already had told her she got to go with us tonight, so she's going to be quite sad. But I'm thankful Dr. Pui is keeping such a close eye on her, and who can argue with the top cancer doctor in the world?

CHAPTER 3
OUR NEW HOME

Day 10, Jan 4, 2011 6:56am
Yesterday was a very scary and emotional day for me. I decided not to journal because I really want to keep this as real as possible, but also as positive as I can, and yesterday I was feeling sorry for myself and for my family. That is definitely NOT the right kind of attitude to have or energy I want to surround Lucy with.

Dr. Pui put Lucy on preventative antibiotics and then said it was up to us if we wanted to come back to the RMH. We asked the nurses if this was normal to put her on these, and they said no. They weren't sure why Dr. Pui was being so cautious with Lucy because her blood work looked good, and yes her antibody level is at zero, but so are other kids at this stage and they don't get sent out with these meds. But, they said Dr. Pui must have an instinct, and he is never wrong.

Wow! Never wrong. They said he would never let us leave if he thought something was unusual though, and he did. They said this whole stay, he's paid extra attention to her. The staff has been great and has just fallen in love with her. She had so many visitors yesterday from nurses to other specialist we had seen the week prior, we thought something was wrong, and they said, "No, we just needed to see Miss Lucy today." Love that they call her Miss Lucy. The South definitely has manners that I'm not quite used to. Usually they came because they wanted her to sing for them.

So last night was scary. They sent us home with a ton of meds, and today we get training on how to give her meds through her port. We also have strict instructions if she has a fever to get back ASAP. Children on chemo can die within an hour of a fever if it's infection. Talk about me freaking out! I guess that's why we are so close to the hospital. Today is day 8 of our protocol and the nasty chemo day (not that they aren't all nasty, but this is double nasty), we are up and off bright and early to start a long day.

Day 10, Jan 4, 2011 11:32pm

Today started at 7 am and is just now winding down at 11 pm; I think that's what time it is. It was our first day of outpatient care, so it was all new. First we registered her, then we got our schedule for the day, then daddy got a quick lesson in how to access her port, clean it out, and give meds through the IV. Then we had to go get the needle taken out of her port and a new one put in. That was a nightmare.

It probably was just scary to her because "buddy" has never had to be messed with like that before. It was an hour and a half of blood-curdling screams and uncontrollable crying. When it was over, I lost it. I couldn't stop crying. Definitely calling my doctor tomorrow for some medication to help me cope better. Zach is doing great. I am so thankful for him and am glad every day I met him. He not only takes care of Lucy, but me too.

After the port incident, we met with the nurse to go over her daily blood work. Her platelets are a little low, probably getting an infusion tomorrow. But all other work looked good. They like to see the lymphoblasts (abnormal cell masses) gone by day 7, which is a good indicator the chemo is killing the cancer. And hers were gone! Yay! After that, Dr. Pui decided not to give her one strong chemo called Dauno. And let us go home until 6 at night and come back for our Vincristine (another double nasty chemo).

Man, you should see our room! We have a mini hospital, and all the supplies are insane. It's a crash course in nursing school! But it's ok, because by teaching us all of this, she is able to be with us here at the RMH. She is still pretty mad about not going home-home, but hopefully, when we get Jack here, that will help.

I went grocery shopping since the little Prednisone girl eats like a 12-ton gorilla. Took me an hour, $100, and I hardly came home with anything. Her diet is so strict. The more processed the food, the better in her case, to ensure no bacteria, but she's also on low sodium. Know how hard that is to do? It's like an oxymoron really. The reason food is so safe when it's processed is due to the sodium!! Then, let's talk about meal preparation.

I totally forgot to re-wash our pan before cooking her tater tots, so that was an epic fail. Even if we wash something in the dishwasher, we have to rewash since we share a kitchen with four other families. We don't know if they have touched anything. So, she had baked lays instead! And no dip, which she wasn't pleased with. No sour cream allowed. No raisins, no tea, and no rice. Those foods are naturally filled with bacteria, and for a normal person with a healthy immune system, it would be fine; for her it can be life threatening and cause an infection due to low immune system.

After dinner, we had to do meds: 4 PO (by mouth), and 2 through her IV. Then we had to give her a sitz bath and cover her bottom with a butt cream I had to make. Then temps and last lotion. She even has prescription lotion because anything petroleum-based can harbor and grow bacteria. This low bacteria thing is totally insane.

So tomorrow is more blood work and that's all that is on our schedule, of course things change by the hour here....

Day 11, Jan 5, 2011 10:09am
Good news for this morning. All we have to do is get platelets, then we get to go back to RMH and don't have to come back till Friday! Yay!

Day 12, Jan 6, 2011 5:22pm
Yesterday was a "short" day. We were done at the hospital by 2, and Lucy got the day off today. You'd think we would have time, but we don't. Meds take up to 5 hours a day, and now we have start taking care of our living space here. Oh, and I drove a long 5 hours one way and picked up Jack. It was so good to see him. He held on to me so tight. I can't imagine what he has been thinking. I started crying and didn't want to let go of him. Now we are a family of four again! The only one missing is Taco ;)

She was stoked to see him, but within an hour, they were fighting. The Prednisone makes her a very angry little girl and Jack doesn't quite understand that yet. Plus he is a little confused because he thinks she's getting tons of presents and all our attention. I am going to aim to spend as much 1x1 with him as possible.

Yesterday a coworker sent Lucy two Beatles movies. 'Help' and 'A Hard Day's Night'. She was screaming like a school girl while watching them. It was good to see her happy for a while. She has started to walk with a limp, and can no longer run. We asked the doc what it was, and it could be several things. It could be atrophy from lying in bed a week, and it could be an effect from the chemo. After treatments are over, it's not unusual for kids to do physical therapy. She can't do her ballet, and that makes me sad.

I want to thank folks for sending packages. The kids love getting mail! And it's a nice surprise for our day.

Day 12, Jan 6, 2011 7:15pm
So we thought today would be slower paced since we weren't at the hospital all day. We were wrong. We had to do laundry, clean our room, and still give Lucy her meds, which I mentioned before take a total of 5 hours through the day. Then of course meal preparation and had to run to Wal-Mart for staples. And now that we have Jack here, we have more responsibility.

I am not complaining, I love him here, but it's got its own stressors. For example, he is really upset and thinks Lucy is getting all kinds of presents and lots of attention. I don't think he understands everything fully. Then we had a conversation last night, and he was talking about how he has been practicing washing his hands and has stopped picking his nose so he doesn't catch Lucy's cancer bugs. I had to explain that it wasn't about preventing him from getting sick, but rather helping her to NOT get sick.

And then there is Lucy on Prednisone. He keeps asking me why she is so grumpy. And she is. She is split personality. Happy at one minute, crying another. I used to get stressed out over it, but today and tonight, I have tried to ignore it. I know she is sick, and it is hard to discipline her, but we have to keep it normal. And she is just plain disrespectful and hateful, and in our house, that is a rule breaker. And now we don't have just one child to cater to, so she needs to learn to share and take turns again. Taking some getting used to, that is for sure.

She is having a hard time walking, and that is sad. I noticed when we first got here that a lot of the kids walked with limps. It can be the chemo. And there is a lot of nerve pain with the chemo, so she complains all the time about something hurting. It's very nerve wracking. Not sure whether to call the nurse, take her in, or give it time. We call. They give us pointers, and tell us what to look for. She also started getting a runny nose today. :(

I'm super scared because a cold can put her in the hospital again. And we have been so careful, but when we go to the hospital and there are hundreds of people there, mask or no mask, you run a risk of catching things. I also don't want her to be sick for Tuesday, which is our big day. They won't do the aspiration if she is sick. and we are already on pins and needles as it is.

Tomorrow we have quite few appointments and are going to take Jack with. He is going to have to learn how to deal with this and see what goes on. Should be interesting trying to keep two kids entertained. I have to say I do feel much, much better having the 4 of us here. I feel like I am in more control. In reality, I have none at all! But it feels that way. And for now, I'll take that.

Sometimes, I sit and still can't believe this has happened and is happening. I am always thinking positively, but there are moments I am scared of what may happen if they can't cure her. I try to get the thoughts out of my head as fast as they come in and have to admit that I am ashamed I even think them. And living at the RMH doesn't help sometimes. There are kids way sicker than Lucy whose parents say they are just buying a little more time. And there is a lady across the hall whose 7-month-old was taken out of here via emergency, and his little body was lifeless. I'm not sure what happened, and I started to cry. I hope he is ok. It's scary.

I was talking to another mom, and we were saying how we thought after the baby phase was over, all was good. After the scare of SIDS, we felt like we could cruise with an occasional flu or infection. I have to honestly say I NEVER thought this would happen. And it's amazing how far they have come for a cure, but still don't have the slightest idea what causes leukemia. They say it's a combination of nature/nurture. It's like your genetic makeup has a tendency to make one bad cell, and then there is something in the environment that triggers it. But what genetic makeup that is, they still don't know, and what environmental factor... no clue. They have seen people of all socioeconomic levels, color, age, and sex with no common bonds at all get leukemia. They have seen twins both get it, and one just get it. Sigh.....

Day 14, Jan 8, 2011 6:05am
Ahhh...the weekend. And we actually get the weekend "off". No doctors. I can't believe I am up so early, but I really like a few minutes to myself... that is a rarity. Zach is the late bird, and I am the early bird. Now if we can get the kids to actually sleep like they do at home, this could work out ok.

Yesterday was pretty hard on me. I think after having Thursday off and then going back, it was just very emotional because Thursday seemed almost normal. I mean, besides the IV meds we had to give and constant checking of fever, it was normal. I wasn't scared all day, we were busy doing household and family things. Then Friday, we pull up to the hospital and the anxiety sets in almost immediately.

Jack went with us too for the first time, so that was interesting. He kept saying, "I'm bored, this is boring, I am ready to go, when we going to go..." the whole 3 hours. That made me realize two things: 1. Bring more than just a DS for the kid and 2. Lucy has never complained about the waiting. She just sits on my lap while I rock her, which shows how sick she must feel. I mean I know I hear her tell me everything hurts, and I know she has leukemia, but for the 3-year-old on Prednisone not to complain, breaks my heart. I can't wait for her to start complaining about waiting.

When we got in the chemo room, the nurses brought the Legos. I also probably am not going to win 'Parent of the Year Award' for yelling at Jack yesterday. He and Lucy were fighting over a stupid toy and he hit her. I smacked his hand and yelled at him so bad. :(Right now we are under a fall risk and so hitting is obviously not good for her, and he got her good. At home, she would have hauled off and hit him back, probably harder than he hit her. But she just cried. Then Jack cried. Then I cried.

I told him that he cannot do that, and if he does it again, he may not be able to stay up here with us. Probably not the best, understanding thing to say to him. Sometimes I forget the kid is only 5; he's so dang smart and independent. Today, I plan on taking just him to do something. And I will apologize. And Monday when we go back to the hospital, I will get one of the child psychologists to come talk to him.

Living in the Ronald McDonald House is becoming "normal". Sharing a kitchen with 4 other families, and taking turns making coffee in the morning, learning about the game room, craft room, etc. has become comforting. I will admit, there are some strange people here that I don't understand. People that steal food from others, steal the donated movies, games, etc. I mean really...stealing from the cancer patients...what the hell is wrong with people? Then, local people come here and stay in rooms with friends and raid the free food cabinets and fridges. Not everybody is like that, but you have your few and you learn quickly who they are.

Then, there are some wonderful friendships we are making. There is one family who has a 4.5 year old and 2 year old, and I swear they live just like we do. Their 4 year old has a brain tumor wrapped around his brain stem. And he and Lucy are so much alike, it's scary. They both love the Beatles. How odd and comforting.

The parents are the same age as us and have similar professions and similar sense of humor. Which is not easy to find!! So I have been talking to the mom a lot. That helps. They got their first "date night" last night since her parents came to watch the kids for the night. It's been their first since they have been here. The mom said she cried through dinner since she was so happy.

I can't wait till I can have a date night with Zach. Heck, we can't wait to have an hour alone to just talk. We text a lot! In the same room, and texting. Ha! But there are things we don't necessarily want to bother the kids with, and we need to communicate somehow.

So with two days off, we shall see if we can keep the kids entertained. Wouldn't be as hard if Lucy could leave the room, but she has to stay in there, unless she is eating, due to risk of infection.

I want to thank everybody for the packages. The kids LOVE getting mail, and the toys and activities have helped out. They both had to leave all their x-mas gifts not even 24 hours after they opened them. I am thankful that we got to have a normal x-mas before this started.

Day 14, Jan 8, 2011 7:54pm
Today we had a bit of a scare. Zach was cleaning up lunch and turned to throw something in the garbage, and some guy in another kitchen gave Lucy a strawberry. UGH! She cannot have that because they are filled with bacteria. She took a nibble, but it still scared us. We called the doc and he said to watch for fever and diarrhea. I have a cousin whose child is allergic to pretty much everything, and I now know what nightmare she lives.

First, why would you even offer food to a kid you don't know with how many allergies are out there nowadays? And second, these people are on low bacteria diet too!! Why are they allowing their children to eat these things??? We explained to Lucy what to say if somebody offers her food again. I think we scared her... but hey, this only took 5 seconds, so it's important.

We also had somebody leave old nasty rice in our kitchen, which is another HUGE no! Tea and rice they say are the deadliest. And this family has a child with same diet at Lucy. I don't get it.

I was looking through Lucy's treatment plan, and thought I would share the specifics and timeline now that I am able to understand it better since I have been getting sleep. First phase is called Remission Induction. Goal: Put the cancer in remission. This lasts 6-7 weeks. This is what we are in now and this is the nastiest part of chemo. Day one is when she got three drugs in her spinal tap and they are the strongest: Methotrexate, Hydrocortisone, and Ara-C.

Days 1-28 she takes Prednisone every day. On days 1, 8, 15, and 22, she gets Vincristine. This is the drug that is mostly responsible for hair loss and it causes her a lot of bone pain. Days 1 and 8, she gets Dauno. And on day 3 she gets Peg Asparaginase, which is another really nasty chemo. Based on her spinal tap results on day 15, she may need it again. On day 22 she gets Cyclophosphamide, and days 23-35 she gets Thioguanine. We aren't at that phase for the last two drugs, so we aren't sure of their side effects yet, and how Lucy may/may not react.

Second phase is called Consolidation. This lasts for 8 weeks, and it will consist of us traveling back and forth from Memphis every 10 days, and her stay here is dependent upon how she reacts to the chemo, and how fast she can pass it through her system.

Third phase is Continuation. This lasts 120 weeks and it will have two phases of the Induction period intermingled in there where we will have to come back to Memphis for a 2-6 week period twice. So, that is our formal treatment if all goes well. It can change based on reactions and fevers, and how Lucy feels.

Man, I knew being a stay-at-home mom was a full time job; I never doubted that. But being a stay home mom and dad with a child with chemo is like having a full time job, two part time jobs, and seasonal work. We get up on week days around 5am. We have to take Lucy to bathroom where she pees in a hat, then we check her pee with some sticks to see if there is glucose in there. Then, if she poops, we have to put her in a sitz bath, make a homemade butt cream for her tush, then get her and Jack dressed.

Then, find Lucy's mask and take them down for breakfast. I have to re-wash any dishes I am about to use to prepare for breakfast, and Zach usually takes Clorox wipes to clean the table and chairs we will be eating off of. I cook breakfast while washing my hands every time I touch anything (my hands are so dry). Then we eat and come back upstairs to take 8 o'clock meds. That is a nightmare.

She still cries and screams for meds. And the morning and night are 4 meds, so they take the longest. And of course, we have to keep Jack at bay during this time. After meds, we pack a bag for the hospital and rush downstairs to catch the 7:30 shuttle to make our 8 appt.

When we get to the hospital, we check in at assessment and triage. We wait. After our name is called, we go back and get weight and vitals. Then they draw blood from "buddy" and do any dressing and needle changes. Again, depending upon what needs to be done, this can take up to an hour.

We wait again after that until the blood work is back, and we meet with Dr. Pui. If she has chemo on the schedule, we do that. And based on blood work, she may have to get blood or platelets. During all the waiting, one of us will go to patient services to get her a coupon for a "snack pack". It is a bag filled with snacks while we are at the hospital all day and friendly for her diet.

Sometimes we may go talk to our social worker, or pick up meds and home supplies. And if all is good with test and meds, we can come back home. Sometimes it is 2 pm, and sometimes its 4 pm. So if it's the earlier, we do our 2 pm meds, lunch (repeating same steps for prep as breakfast), and then nap. We get up from nap, and start same prep for dinner. While dinner is cooking, one of us does our laundry (we have at least 2 loads a day to keep the room manageable). Then, we clean our room after dinner and before the 2 IV meds and oral meds at 7 and 8. All while keeping Jack entertained. Some nights are real baths with hair being washed and covering her with lotion because her skin is more dry than mine. Then we can finally sit back and remember all the things we forgot to do for the day!! LOL! Some days, we squeeze in grocery shopping or settling things back home. I cannot imagine only one of us taking care of all this. It definitely takes a team.

I also have to say that having Jack here is helping. I don't notice her fits as much. I'm not sure if she isn't having them as much, or if I just have learned to tune them out already! Ha! And Jack is very caring to her most of the time; there are times, like last night, that he too gets frustrated. She did say tonight, "I am so glad Jack is here." And I am too; he is such a good cuddler.

Tomorrow is another day "off". Maybe we can do another fun activity like today. I took the kids to the craft room, and we made aquariums, puppets, and painted. Maybe tomorrow we can play some family games.

Day 15, Jan 9, 2011 9:08pm
Today, I got to spend some much needed time with Jack. We went to Target and then out for lunch. I was trying to give him 100% of my attention, but deep in my stomach, I felt guilty for leaving Lucy. At lunch, he told me, "Mom, it's fun hanging out just you and me." That pretty much made me focus on him, and then we were sitting in a booth, and he looks up and says, "I'd like to sit next to you". So we did. We had a fun lunch telling jokes and shooting toothpicks at the ceiling (it was allowed there).

On the way home, he asked me if he will always remember Lucy when he gets older.

I said, "What do you mean?"

He said, "Well, will I always know her and see her in Heaven?"

I said, "Honey, do you think Lucy is going to die? Are you scared?"

He said, "No, I know she isn't going to die, but I wonder how it will be when we get older."

I'm not sure where he was going with that conversation, but I felt bad for him. He's processing something, and I can't quite get it out of him yet, so I can't help him or talk to him.

Lucy had a rough day today. Tired and wanting to spend it in bed. She would get up for 5 minutes, then be wiped and ready to go back to bed. She ate a lot though: chicken noodle soup with crackers for breakfast and lunch and 5 pieces of pizza and 4 breadsticks for dinner!!! And then she was complaining her stomach hurt. Well, no wonder.

She was asking about her hair again today, and it's starting to fall out. When you brush it or run your fingers through it, it comes out. So I think it is time for the short haircut. She said that was cool as long as she looked like "John from the Beatles." :)

Tonight I was on pins and needles. Her temp was close to the 100.4 mark at 100.1. If it hits the 100.4, she gets three days inpatient automatically and that is if nothing is wrong. Which would mean no day 15 procedure and they may delay chemo. We have to check it periodically throughout the day. Usually a kiss on the forehead from me will tell me whether or not to take it. We retook it an hour later and it was 99. It goes up and down so quickly because of meds. So you can imagine, its "pins and needles"

Speaking of meds, talk about a nightmare. She screams bloody murder and you can hear her throughout the entire house. We even put her meds in Hershey's chocolate syrup, and she still freaks out. She pulls out every stall tactic she can think of. To name a few: I have to go potty, my lip hurts, I need Chapstick, I need a break after that one, etc., etc., etc. It was funny in the beginning, but now it's a fact that she will have to become accustomed to.

She has meds 3 times a day. Although, I don't feel so bad when she screams because there are a lot of other children on steroids throwing tantrums as well. Makes us feel "normal". And it's funny how everybody goes about conversations and day to day things as our children are throwing tantrums and screaming till their faces turn red. You do get used to it; I would have never guessed that. And you can tell the new parents who are in there because they apologize for their steroid child throwing a fit.

I seem to just be rambling tonight with no specific path or thought; I think I have had time to get some of my to-do list done, so my brain is fried. It was nice to have the day off, but I am anxious for Tuesday and having a hard time concentrating. I really want to know her prognosis. I want to know her odds.

I have met another family from Bloomington who also work at State Farm. They are in their 3rd phase of treatment, so it was nice to chat with her, and see how relaxed she is. She said she didn't used to be and that she used to be a basket case (like me), but it gets better after the Induction phase. I hope so. Never knew how many people from Illinois had leukemia until we got here. They have hand prints all over the RMH of kids who have some sort of cancer. It lists their DOB and date of diagnosis along with where they are from. You would not believe how many folks are from our area. Matter of fact, majority of people on the walls are from Illinois and Louisiana. I wonder if there is a study about that.

Tomorrow is a short day (barring no fever in the middle of the night), so daddy is going to take her in tomorrow, while Jack and I stay here to clean our room (AGAIN) and do laundry. It is tight quarters to say the least.

This evening we had both kids throwing fits. It was lovely. I think sometimes we need separation. And sometimes Zach and I would KILL for a moment alone. After Tuesday, we will know if visitors could come down starting next weekend. Of course with no runny noses, colds or ANYTHING! LOL

Day 16, Jan 10, 2011 3:49pm
Ok, we got our schedule for tomorrow; I'm so nervous and ready. We go in at 10 for labs, then we wait until 11 to go see Pui to find out if there is anything preventing her from getting a spinal tap. At 12:30, she gets ready to go in for surgery, which will be done by 2. She has to sit in recovery for an hour, then from 4-5, we have to go and get her "buddy" changed. We probably won't find out until Wednesday if there is any leukemia left in her blood.

They shoot for less than 5% left. They really want 0, but that is rare. Whatever the percent is will determine how strong her doses of chemo will be. Even though they may have killed it, her body still is "confused" and will continue to make the cancer cells. That is why she will continue chemo until it keeps killing and killing and killing ANY cells and any hiding cells, and it will also teach her body to stop making them. It is like after getting killed so much, the cancer cells stop being produced because they are tired of losing. I know that is very simple layman's terms, but it's the best and easiest way for me to explain it.

We have been waiting for this day because it will tell us if her body is reacting to chemo, and if not, what our other plan of action may be. The bad thing is, she cannot eat after midnight tonight. That is going to be the toughest on us. Not allowing her to eat will be painful. And having Jack with us all day at the hospital will be rough as well. I am packing his backpack with lots of activities tonight. Then we are going to have to feed him secretly; not looking forward to that aspect of the day.

So there is a bug or virus going around the RMH. We were informed it would be best to stay in our room for everything. Which we are. They said some folks had visitors who brought it in. Again, I do not understand people. Then the people we share our kitchen with, and who we are having problems with, have left rice out twice, and now there is raw chicken sitting in a pan for 2 days so far. UGH. Zach inquired about moving to the Target house, which is private apartments, but they only do those for long-term patients. Doesn't hurt to ask, especially since there are 2 families here who have been here for 7 years and 4 years, respectively, who don't want the Target house. I said "we will take your spot". :) The apartments have two bedrooms, separate living space, your own kitchen, etc.

Man, if anybody has ANY pull, could you hook us up to live at the Target house???? LOL

Day 17, Jan 11, 2011 8:06am
Ok, today is our first milestone. I will keep everybody posted as we find out results. May take til tomorrow, but I'll let you know how she does in surgery.

She's already up and crying because she can't eat. We will take all the positive thoughts and prayers you can muster today!!!

Day 17, Jan 11, 2011 12:58pm
We are waiting on our blood work, and then we will head back to get ready for surgery. I'm so nervous and on edge, I feel like I'm going to burst into tears. I hope like mad her marrow test comes back negative, meaning zero cancer left.

We have already been prepared that next Tuesday will be a 12-hour chemo day here at the hospital. Going to be rough for Jack!! May have to do shifts. Then after that, we have heard we will have to give antibiotics in the middle of the night. That's going to go over well.

We start a new drug today that she will take for the next 2.5 years to prevent her from getting a certain pneumonia. She will be pleased to add another medicine to her regimen! Ha!

As for Lucy, besides being hungry, she's in good spirits today. Fighting with Jack and telling him to share, and telling the nurses and Dr. Pui fart jokes, lovely! My sweet lady-like daughter!! Hahaha!!

Day 17, Jan 11, 2011 9:39pm
We will get results tomorrow to see how much cancer is left in Lucy's bone marrow. Today was a rough day on everybody.

Hoping for sleep to come so tomorrow can get here quicker.

I had, and am having, my first real breakdown since this all started. Can't seem to stop crying. Not sure what triggered it; pretty sure Lucy's hair falling out really bad now had something to do with it. I know that sounds so vain, but really it just makes her disease more visible. Of course both children tell me "It's ok, mama, everything's going to be ok".

At lunch today, Jack asked me why I looked so sad. He said, "Are you scared?" This is while Lucy was in surgery. I told him that yes, I was scared. He said, "Mom, don't worry, the doctors will take good care of her." And even before surgery, he was in her room with us and standing right by her bed and holding her hand. Such a sweet boy.

So after surgery, Lucy had to get chemo. What a grand day for her! As we were waiting for her chemo, she had a "roid rage" (that's what we call steroid fits). Then they called our name for chemo and it was chaotic. After we got in the chemo room, we realized Jack left his DS case in the waiting room, so we went to get it because it had his games in it. When we got there, it was gone. Somebody stole it. What a shitty day made even shittier! Poor guy. We got back to the room, and Jack has been complaining that his stomach hurts and that he doesn't feel good. He said he better go home. I think this is a bit much for him.

So I'm torn on what to do. I don't want to leave her for one second, but I can't send him home without a parent. I think he needs routine, plus it's really hard having a new set of responsibilities with another child up here, and not sure it's fair to him to come in 2nd all the time. That could be why I'm so upset too.

Day 18, Jan 12, 2011 5:16am
I am up bright and early, although I am tired as heck. It's like x-mas morning when you are waiting to see what you got, so you can't sleep. That is how I feel about these test results. It's not like getting up any earlier is going to make them process any faster. :)

The one thing I love about getting up early, besides alone time, is the 3rd shift security guard. He rocks. He makes coffee every morning when he works. AND the coffee is McDonald's coffee. Not sure if you are aware, but McDonald's actually has good coffee.

Another common thing I wake up to every morning is a stuffy nose and even a bloody nose here and there. St. Jude, RMH, and Target House are equipped with special air filtration systems. They pretty much clean the air over and over and over and over. Bad thing -- it makes the air so dry, which is what they want. Humid air is where bacteria grow. But my poor nose could use some humidity right now. They use HEPA filters in each room, and that is what they say we should do when we get home too. So, now we get to update our furnace and vents as well as water system. :)

I don't know if I already mentioned this or not, but I find it so weird that every article that I read about leukemia starts out with "fortunately, childhood cancer is rare." And I understand when they are looking at the numbers, it is in fact a minority, but when you are in the midst of it here, it's not so rare. We realize how lucky we are that Lucy got the kind of the cancer she has. Zach was teasing and saying, "If you are gonna get cancer, THIS is the one you want." It is so true. We are so fortunate to have an overall good prognosis, a treatment plan that they are tweaking and proving works, and Lucy who is still able to walk around and play. Isn't that sad? We feel lucky because she got a "better" cancer. UGH. Never thought I'd say that

There are lots of kids here with tumors, who lose their ability to walk or may lose a limb. Then you have the retinoblastoma children (cancer of the retina). They have a great prognosis; if the cancer is only in one eye, they just remove their eye. After it spreads to the other eye, they try not to remove both eyes, but if it is at risk for spreading outside the retina, they have to. Once it spreads, the prognosis for living is less than 5%. There is also another little girl, same age as Lucy, who as ALL T-Cell (there are two types), and she started her treatments the same time, and she is already in a wheelchair and cannot walk. The T-cell kids have to get double the lumbar punctures that Lucy gets. The T-cell has a higher risk for recurrence. And she is the sweetest thing with this curly, curly hair. So like I said, we are fortunate to have what we have. That includes our family and friends and all the support. There are a lot of people here who don't have any of that.

Zach and I already said that when this is all said and over with, we definitely have a new bill every month to make sure we pay first. And that is our donation to St. Jude and the RMH. I never realized how many awesome things they do, and truthfully, I never bothered to look it up. Why would I? And that sounds self-serving because it is. Out of sight, out of mind. My mom gives to St. Jude every month, and in December she didn't send her check, so we plan on teasing her relentlessly that if she had sent her check, this wouldn't have happened ;) (just teasing mom).

So the nice family we met, whose son also likes the Beatles, and he has the brain tumor, gets to go home today! Yea for them!! She said, "But we will be back in 3 weeks to start chemo." She asked for my contact information, and I said, "We will still be here in three weeks when you come back!" And that is so true. Depressing and necessary, but true.

Zach also met a mom who is a hairdresser... thank god! I can't stand to see Lucy's hair all over her shirts, blankets, and pillows. So today we are going to get her a haircut. ;) We are going for a "Twiggy" haircut. Short and chic. Then as it falls out more, we will shave it. But I told Zach that I didn't want to go straight for the bald yet. I'm not ready.

We absolutely love Lucy's doctor. He has a lousy bedside manner with parents, which drives Zach up the wall because he's trying to "crack" him by telling bad jokes! LOL!! But, he is wonderful with Lucy and Jack. He told Lucy the other day, "Good thing you only have 2 legs and not 4. In China, we eat anything that has 4 legs." Then when he came to see her yesterday and realized that her appointment for surgery was so late in the day, he went OFF on the nurse! Poor nurse. He said. "That baby cannot wait to eat that long and that now we won't get results until the next day."

So he is an even bigger advocate for her than we are. We have questions or problems, we tell Pui, and he makes it better, or at least tries to make it better. Pui also did one of her procedures yesterday, so he had come in and Lucy said, "Dr. Pui, you have already seen me today, what are you doing back?" He got a kick out of that.

Today is supposed to be a day "off" again. Unless the MRD (Minimal Residual Disease) test comes back bad, we get to stay here today. That is the test that tells us how much cancer is left. Normally, if it's higher than 5% left, we have to go back for an extra treatment, but Pui said if it comes back higher than 1% with Lucy, he's giving her an extra treatment. He is so cautious with her. At first that scared us, but now we are ok with it because we know he is doing what he thinks is best.

So today I will go to Kroger and get groceries for the week and take along Jack so he can get out of here. Probably be a day of laundry, and we have had a memory game in our room that I am dying to play with the kiddos :) and there is a huge checkers/chess table in the lobby that Jack wants to learn. I also thought I would see if there was a Barnes and Noble nearby so I could buy Jack some of those 1st reader books. He hates to actually read himself, loves stories being read to him, but it's also not his strong point in school (it's math, go figure, like his dad), so that will help him stay on track and will be sure to cause a fit. :)

As soon as I get the results, I will post them to let everybody know. Thank you again for the support, it means the world to all of us!

Day 19, Jan 13, 2011 12:26pm
Quick post to give folks news: We got our results from the MRD. She has .145 cancer left in her blood. So basically they tested 10,000 bone marrow cells and 14 came back positive with cancer. On day one, all 10,000 were positive with cancer. So Dr. Pui said

it's not good, but it's not bad. It's not good enough for him; he wants zero. The nurse said it's great news. So I'm going with that! Lol!

Day 20, Jan 14, 2011 6:31am
Besides getting our test results yesterday, we had some pretty big events happen. Lucy got a haircut, daddy got a haircut, we celebrated Zach's birthday early, and Jack is going home today.

Lucy's hair was starting to fall out too much to be manageable. It was getting in her food and mouth and all over her clothes. So we gave her (actually this other resident of the RMH gave her) a haircut and went short.

It's much curlier short and she likes it a lot. After her bath, we put some gel in it and styled it. She said "I look just like Ringo!" It's much thinner, so not sure how long before we will have to shave it completely. But I couldn't go straight to bald; I needed a step in there.

Her nickname is "hair" if that gives you any indication how much she had!

Jack said, "Lucy, you look like a boy!" We were getting ready to get on him for being rude when Lucy piped up and said, "Good! Then I look just like the Beatles!"

Daddy got a haircut too!! He went bald!! Lucy got to shave it, then mommy helped finish it off. He actually looks pretty good! He kept saying "Are you ok with this? You know it's going to look horrible?"

Jack had the worst time with this. We aren't sure why but he had a major meltdown. Kept saying daddy was going to look creepy. We also had the RMH ask if they could video Lucy cutting daddy's hair for their huge fund raiser coming up. Of course we said yes. This place has provided us with a home and we don't have to worry about anything. While the community living is tough with 2 kids (Not like college where you just partied!! At least I did! Ha!), it's still comforting to have a place to call our own. We told a little bit about our story, so I'll keep you posted when and where to tune in to that!

We celebrated daddy's birthday early (it's actually Sunday) because, as I mentioned, Jack is going home today. I made a cake, and Jack helped me decorate it. And we are big on birthdays in our family, so it was complete with Phineas and Pherb (I have no idea how to spell either of those! Jack picked them out) decorations.

Jack had a major meltdown Wednesday night. He said he missed home and his bed and he wondered if his Legos were even still there. He said he wanted to go back to school and it was too hard to be up here. I told him if he went home, mommy and daddy wouldn't be able to go with him. He said, "One can stay here with Lucy and the other can go home with me." I told him that during this first phase of treatment that was not possible.

So I had the counselor talk to him yesterday. She said Jack was very good at expressing his feeling and that he had a good understanding of what was going on for his age. She said for kids his age, out of sight means potentially gone. So he wanted to see us so bad because he needed that proof we were still here. He did relay to her that the last thing he remembered about me before we left for Memphis was mommy getting in the ambulance with Lucy and crying really hard. I hadn't realized he had seen that.

Anyhow, now that he knows where we are at, he got a tour of the hospital, he knows what they are doing for Lucy, and he now needs to make sure his home is still there. Makes sense. Poor kid hasn't seen it since we left the morning after x-mas. And the counselor said it would good for him and that he expressed that is what he really wants. So I'm taking him home today.

My mom is going to stay at our house with him and get him off to school. And I will come visit when I can. We will be in Memphis at least another 4 weeks, as long as there are no infections, fevers, or complications. Then we will get to come home for 10 days efore

36

coming back for 2-3 days.

We are leaving as soon as Zach and Lucy leave for their appointment this morning, and then I will try to take care of some business back home and return Monday. I hate leaving Lucy, but Jack needs this so I want to be sure he doesn't feel like 2nd class, which I know he has the past few days.

CHAPTER 4
LIVING WORLDS APART

Day 21, Jan 15, 2011 12:35am
I have no idea why I am up at midnight! I fell asleep around 9 in
my own bed with Taco, but have to admit it doesn't feel quite
right without Zach, and of course I'm worried I am too far away
from Lucy if anything happens.

Jack, on the other hand, is THRILLED to be home. First thing he
did was go straight to his room and play for about an hour with
his Legos. He said, "Mom, all my stuff is still here." Poor kid. I
asked if he missed Daddy and Lucy being home and he said, "No,
cuz Lucy and I would just be fighting." LOL !

I think the grumpiness and lack of energy Lucy had got to the
little fella. He wants normalcy, and this is how he thinks it should
be. He did share with me that he is excited for "little" grandma to
come over here and take care of him when I go back because, and
I quote, "She lets me do whatever I want." HAHAHAHA!!!
Busted, mom! Oh, he calls my mom "little grandma" and Zach's
mom is "big grandma". He started doing that all on his own when
he was tiny. We aren't sure why because my mom is taller than
Theresa, so we concluded it must be due to the size of their
houses. Mine is in a small apartment, and Zach's in a big farm
house.

Of course, I told him I was writing rules down that must be
followed while we are gone or else I will have grandma mail me
his DS to the RMH. He had a look of shock and horror. I feel bad
because I kind of yelled at him when we got home. I told him that
I understood he was feeling bad and that things weren't easy, but
his behavior had to change now that we were home. I told him he
could not be disrespectful to his parents and that his manners had
to get better. We were lax on the punishments while at RMH
because it's hard to discipline your kid in front of 100 other
families! LOL! And how do you send a kid to time out who is
living in a shoebox with no toys anyhow? Plus, he has been

talking back, and he doesn't do that very often. So, I'm sure this is his way of expressing his feelings for the situation, but he will have to learn to do it a different way.

Zach and I always joked when we became parents that we knew we would screw our kids up somehow, and that we would pay for their first 5 therapy sessions. Now we say we better extend that to the first 10! Ha! Seriously, probably going to have to do some family sessions once we get home and things are settled.

I think the thing Jack was most excited about was his bed and routine. I told him it was relaxing time so to get his PJs on, and he was all about it. We usually let them watch a short show like 'The Simpsons' (I know awesome children programming at its very best), then we do a book and then bed. We haven't had routine in over 3 weeks, so he LOVED it, and went straight to bed. I thought he would ask to sleep with me, but he didn't. I would have let him, :(but didn't want to offer and start bad habits.

Taco is home! Yea!!! I have to say, he didn't look so sure of himself when he got here. Of course Jack zeroed in on him in full attack mode, and I'm sure he was thinking "Oh, please let me go back to the place with no kids." HAHAHA!!! He crashed on the couch most of the night and was snoring he was sleeping so soundly. Although, before Uncle Denny left (that is where he got to stay, we call it the Shangri-La for dogs) he looked at Denny like "please take me with you." At bed time, he was burrowing under the covers, like he normally does, and he couldn't quite get settled. I couldn't either. I love our bed, and it's probably worth more than anything else we own outright, but it's awfully big when you are in it alone.

Normally, I would KILL to be in there alone; not tonight. I slept in the middle, thinking that would help, and Taco really likes to sleep in between Zach and I, so he kept searching for that extra body to snuggle up to. Probably going to have to pay for the dog whisperer therapy too!

It is good to be home. It's familiar. Weird, but familiar. Our cleaners had come while we were gone, so the house looked GREAT!! Thank god for them. And compared to the room at the RMH, this place is HUGE!! It's like a mansion. We call it our vacation home now. ;) We used to complain how tiny it was. Perspective...

Lucy and daddy had a good day today. It basically consisted of her getting checked out at the hospital. No blood work or anything. Just had to get vitals. And Dr. Pui lowered her blood pressure meds because she is doing so well. And then she ate all day. And I mean ALL day. You should check out pictures on Facebook if you haven't already. I can't upload some of them on here because they are too big, but let me tell you! Her cheeks are so huge and chubbilicious. Yes, that is a word. She eats like it's the end of the world. Which is good, and quite funny, but she gets demanding.

Prednisone causes cravings, and that girl craves stuff we didn't even know she knew about!! Ha! Lots and lots of pasta and carbohydrates, which we have to watch because if she gets too much glucose in her urine, we will then be on a low carb, low sodium, low bacteria diet, and the girl won't be able to eat anything!

Tuesday, we start her long chemo day, it's over 12 hours. But we also start week 4, so two more to go after that for Induction and Phase 1 will be over! Yea!! We will start Phase 2 in Memphis, then depending on how she does, get to come home for 10 days. And yes, I AM planning now!!! I have it marked on my calendar!!! I have the entire treatment marked as tentative dates.

I think that is the hardest part about me being home and why I can't sleep. She's not here. And it's hard to look in her room and at the life we left when we scrambled out of here in a hurry that day. Two weeks prior to us finding this out, our lives were normal. I found her birthday cards lying on the counter, and it made me sad. Also looking at Jack's school folder, and lists of to-dos. They were so important, and now they are so trivial. And our computer screen has all our pictures flash as a screen saver, and whenever I see hers come up when she was a baby, it breaks my heart.

I wish I could take this all away from her. Back here at home, the idea of her having cancer sets in a little bit more than it does at St. Jude. I know that sounds crazy since we are surrounded by cancer there. But there, it's normal. Here, it's not. Here I am reminded of how our life was and how it will never be again. And that's hard. I also have to remember that when I talk to people about childhood cancer, it's new to them and devastating.

Not that it's not devastating for my family, but we are living in the middle of it, and that is what our dinner conversations are about at the RMH. It's like talking about your job or sports activities your children are involved in. I have to remember that here it's different and very emotional and raw for people. So that is one of the good things about being in Memphis. We have a support network on a daily basis. Chemo is a part of our to-do list.

Speaking of to-do lists, I better go ahead and make mine for what I need to do while I am home. Hopefully sleep will come, and if not, there is always a nap later. :)

Day 22, Jan 16, 2011 6:27am
Yesterday was a nice "off" day for me, but Zach and Lucy were plenty busy.
Zach had gone in around 10:30 to the hospital for vital checks only (what they told him), and instead they ended up drawing blood and based on Lucy's hemoglobin numbers decided to give her a transfusion. Those take FOREVER. They had to type the blood since it had been a long time since it was typed. Basically, they have to make sure of what type her blood is, and what antibodies are in there; takes about an hour.

Then they have to match her blood with blood from the donor bank. Even though she is O+, another person's O+ may not necessarily match due to the antibodies, so they have to match it under the microscope to make sure there are no reactions. This takes another hour. Then giving the blood to her takes anywhere from 3-4 hours.

So a trip Zach thought would take an hour, took all day. BUT... the blood helps her perk up and have more energy, so in the long run totally worth it.

The first time they told us she needed a transfusion, we were freaked out. Never had to have that before, so we asked if we could just donate ours, and they explained it takes a long time to clean it and type and match it. Plus they don't recommend parents donate any blood during her entire treatment in case she needs a bone marrow transplant. And if we had given blood within a certain amount of time, we wouldn't be a candidate for a transplant.

Wow, it's amazing how the blood helps her so much. The chemo kills all her red blood cells and platelets, so she needs them regularly, and I want to thank everybody that gives blood and encourage you to do it as often as you are allowed. Sad that until we saw the impact it makes, we kind of didn't think about it much. Man, I'm giving up all our selfish secrets aren't I!!?? :)

Today is Zach's birthday. Hate not being there with him, but today is also my last day with Jack for the next 3-4 weeks unless her ANC gets high enough, then he can come down to visit. I plan on taking him out to breakfast and maybe a movie later. And I want to get Zach a birthday present, but I am struggling with what to give him. If I had my choice, I would give him time :). Time to do whatever he wanted, but that isn't going to be realistic.

Yesterday I got some much needed errands ran and got to see my sister and her family, plus one of my close friends, so that was a nice change. It was good to laugh, and I don't like being alone at home. My mind wanders, and I start to get sad, and I DO NOT want to move to anything but positive thoughts. I also got to cuddle with Taco like it was nobody's business. For those of you who don't know, Taco is our loyal wiener dog who we consider a 3rd child. Who BTW, JUST woke up! It was good therapy to snuggle with him.

Tuesday is our big chemo day. Over 12 hours at the hospital. And it also marks the start of week 4 of Induction. Induction is 6 weeks long, so she is almost through the roughest part of the harshest chemo. Her Prednisone only lasts the first 28 days, and that will end next Monday so maybe her moods will stabilize a little more. But I swear she hasn't had too many "roid rages", and the other attitude is just her.

The nurses would say, "Oh, that is just the medicine" when she would snap at us. Zach and I would say, "You don't know our daughter too well because that is totally normal behavior for her" which I see as her fighting spirit and spunky attitude, and that is what is going to get her through this. So before, when Zach and I would worry how she was going to be as a teenager if she is already like this at 3, we now are grateful for it! Ask me again when she's 13, and I may change my mind ;).

Day 23, Jan 17, 2011 7:25am
Slept a little later than I wanted to! Oops! Wanted to be on the road by 7:30, obviously going to be a bit delayed. I just didn't want to get out of my bed. The first night was hard to sleep there, but last night was pure bliss!! Lol! I think Taco knows something's up because when I brought the packed suitcases out, he wouldn't stop sitting on my lap or being at my heels. Poor guy.

Jack is fine right now with us not being here. I think he is stoked to be home. We shall see after a week or two if he feels the same. It is hard to leave one child, but right now, Lucy needs both of us, and Zach and I need each other. We will be home soon enough, and Jack will wish we would leave again! LOL!

I really appreciated all the emails, calls, texts, and even running into people while I was home. The support is awesome and shows that there are genuine people in this world that want to do good. I'm a cynic by nature, so this is really good to see and very inspiring. Zach and I are still in disbelief and overwhelmed over the outpouring of support. The other thing is the emails from folks we have never met who have battled this. There are so many in our area. That is such a shock. It means the world to me when they say, "everything you are going through sounds very familiar and normal." And when they all say, my child has been cancer free for 5, 10, and even 20 years!!! What great hope!

There are also those out there who give me the pity look or look of great sadness. I hate that look. Yes, this is rough, and yes it is scary. But we will get through it, and Lucy will be stronger for it. So please give us your smiles and tell us your best cancer jokes, and dance and sing to the Beatles while thinking of Lubelle.

What? Don't have any cancer jokes?? Zach does! Hahaha! If you haven't noticed, we are a family who gets through this with laughter. If you give into fear, the cancer wins.

I strongly believe everything happens for a reason, we don't know the reason when it happens, and we question the bad stuff, but in the end, this journey will somehow reach out to somebody else or Lucy will become a doctor or nurse because of it and help people or something!!! Lol!! Not sure what the reason is, but be assured there is one.

And I'm not religious, but am very spiritual. I believe the universe is connected and we have experiences for a good cause. I think there is something bigger than ourselves out there, but that we have control over our fate and choices. Now that doesn't mean I want people to stop praying for Lucy!! I could be wrong! Lol!! And any positive thinking for her, reaches her, and I believe that. So share her story and share her pictures and start your day with a good song from the Beatles!!

Day 24, Jan 18, 2011 8:48am
Today is a new round of chemo and a long day for Lu. It's so long because they give IV fluids before the chemo and after. Then, she starts a new drug that we have to give her at night. She can't have food 2 hours before or 1 hour after; plus they say it works best at night.

She is getting even chunkier, and I have only been away 3 days!! Lol! I gave her a bath and afterwards we put this lotion all over, so when I was done with her, she wanted to do me. She wanted to do my tummy so she was showing me how to lie down and when she tried to get back up she couldn't!! Her tummy is so big, she had to roll. We were both laughing so hard. She said, "My belly is fat like Santa's."

Her hair is literally coming out in clumps. She has bald spots, and we asked if she was ready to get it shaved and go bald, she said no. So we will wait til she is ready. She is also getting good with routine and knowing what her meds are. She will ask before she takes each one: Is this for my heart? Is this for the cancer bugs? Etc., etc.

Last night she didn't sleep so well. Was up crying and yelling. She was hungry. And then she wanted to make sure I would make mac n' cheese and hot dogs for breakfast, which I did. Her appetite is amazing. 3 burrito sized tacos for dinner last night!!! And then a snack later, no wonder her cheeks are so big.

We are getting to know a lot more families. A few are a couple of days ahead of us in protocol and one is a week behind us. This helps. We compare stories and tell them what to expect and vice versa. We are on day 22 today. 6 more days of Prednisone. Then we may move to a stronger steroid, or we may not. It's different for each child. We hope not, the Dex is much worse with fits and rages!!

Last night Lucy's ANC numbers were at 500! It's the first time they have gone up since the chemo and cancer knocked them out. A normal person is around 3000, but we are happy to see hers go up even if for just a day! Lol! The chemo will knock them out again. Basically, it just helps lower her risk of infection when they are higher. And it could be a good sign that they are nice normal healthy white blood cells and not leukemia. We are hoping for remission!!!

Day 25 Jan 19, 2011 6:24am
We made it through our long, long day yesterday, and Lucy was a champ!! We were up at 6 am and in bed by midnight. All day at

the hospital can get on your nerves; Zach and I were a little snippy with one another, but Lucy, as long as she had food, she was good.

We had a minor setback though. We were about an hour 1/2 away from being all done, and Lucy had to go to the bathroom. So I got her up and took her to the bathroom. Mind you, she is all hooked up to two IV's complete with the IV cart. As we were coming back into her room, and I was putting her up on her bed, her IV lines got caught on her bed, so I was trying to untangle them, and then I tripped over the other lines, and pulled her needle out of her "buddy". :(

She was screaming, I was crying...it was not a pretty sight. So the nurse came in and took a look, and the needle had come all the way out and scratched her, so they had to put a new on in. She hates when they mess with buddy. I felt horrible. It's bad enough to see your child go through pain, but when you know you caused it.... UGH!

Anyhow, after it was all said and done and we had a new needle in, she had to go to the bathroom again. She told me she would wait for daddy! LOL! She said, "Mommy, you fall a lot." Then when daddy took her, she asked, "Do you think you cannot step on my buddy like mommy did?" So that definitely lightened the mood. Little booger.

Yesterday, she also got to eat in the cafeteria for the first time, which she LOVED. It was nice for her to get out of the room and do something different than just the RMH.

We also got her schedule for the rest of the Induction phase and the first week of the Consolidation phase. This week through Saturday, she goes in everyday for and IV push of a chemo called Ara-C. Then at night we give her another chemo by mouth for the next 14 days. Then she has Sunday, Monday, and Tuesday off. Monday is also her last day for Prednisone. Then she goes back on Wednesday and gets more Ara-C for 4 days. Then she has a few days off. Then on Tuesday, Feb 1, she gets a whole week

OFF!!!

We have to stay here because her numbers will be low, and the point of this week is to get her numbers up so we can get another bone aspiration to check status of her leukemia, which should be in total remission, and start the next phase of her recovery plan.

If her numbers are good, Feb 8, we will start our consolidation plan. She will get a high dose of Methotrexate, which will require her to be inpatient again for 2-4 days. And if her numbers recover nicely, she will get to go home, home for 10 days. Then we come back every two weeks, so on Feb 22, March 8, and March 22 she will get these treatments. They require inpatient stay, but she gets to come home in between them if her numbers are good. So that is very exciting!!

She is also done with the chocolate syrup in her meds! LOL! She will probably never like chocolate after this is over. She says "Let's just take them without it". The doc has also stopped her IV meds through buddy that we give her at home (antibiotics), so that's a little scary because her numbers will be dropping in the next two days, so risk for infection will be great again. But we have shaved at least 3 hours off our day by not having to administer these. So the next weeks are "light" days; that is if you can call chemo light at all!

I tell you what, Zach and I were commenting last night on her strength because I had just given her a dose of her new chemo she takes by mouth every night. And within in 15 minutes, she was telling us she was so happy, and talking up a storm about food. I got to sleep with her last night, so before bed (mind you its midnight), she was telling me what I needed to get at the store the next day, and what her menu looked like for the next week. When I told her it was time for bed and to be quiet, she was whispering all the different foods to her baby "White"! LOL! I was also telling her last night how proud I was of her. And how she was a strong little girl and very brave. I don't think her smile could have gotten any bigger and she looks at me and says "Mommy, I am so happy".

On the home front, Jack goes back to school today. I hope the routine helps him. He is homesick for us, so today after school, I told him I wanted a phone call. He told my mom he wants to video chat because he likes to see us all. I can't wait to hear how his day goes.

So today will be a short day at the hospital (only 4 hours), and tonight we will see the effects on Lucy of the new chemo. It's different for every child, so hopefully we can keep the upset tummy and nerve pain at a minimum for her. I think I will scrub the room and do the errand running while daddy takes her to her appt.

Day 26, Jan 20, 2011 6:20am
Yesterday was a short day at the hospital for daddy and Lucy only 4 hours. I stayed here and did the cleaning and laundry (never knew we would have so much laundry for just three of us in a day!). Lucy seemed to have a rough morning. Not sure if the chemo was starting to affect her or not, but she actually didn't want to eat. But by time they got back, she was all ready to go and have her lunch.

We also got to video chat with Jack yesterday before his first day back at school, and again when he got home from school, and before bed. He asked when he gets to come back down here. I think he's homesick for one of us. And he brought up a logical argument: He said there are 2 parents, and 2 of us. Why can't one of you be with Lucy and one of you be home with me? He gets that logic from his dad, and the emotion from me. But you know, he is right. As much as both of us want to be here with Lucy, the next couple of weeks are routine, no major procedures, and nothing out of the ordinary. Short hospital visits, and long room stays. So it might actually be best if one of us goes home to be with him for the next 2 weeks. Plus there are things that need to be done to the house to get it ready for her first homecoming.

One of the hardest things lately has been her hair falling out. It comes out in clumps and there are bald spots starting to form at the top of her head. The back is still pretty thick, but also starting to thin. It's very emotional for me, and it's bothersome for her. It's all over her pillows, blankets, food, gets in her mouth, eyes, etc. So we decided to just shave her entire head last night and go bald. She was ok with it.

At first she said it "hurt", and we said what hurts about it? Come to find out, it was the clippers and how loud they were. So we gave her my iPod and sang the Beatles with her while we shaved it. When we got done and she looked at it she said, "Now I look like all the rest of the kids." It was as if she felt like she "belonged." And while she is extra cute with no hair and chubby cheeks, it was very emotional for me. The nurses warned that it was usually hard on mom the most, and they were right. It just solidified the fact that she is sick. I cried for about 2 hours last night down stairs.

The physical changes and emotional changes are hard for me. I am searching for that little girl on x-mas morning, and she is fading. She is now full of medical terms, procedures, no real "friend" interaction since we have to stay in our room if we aren't in the hospital. Her normal energy is gone, and even her voice has changed. I know this is all necessary in order to be cured, but I worry about what this does to her free spirit. Zach says I worry too much. I just can't wait for the day when she is home and playing with her babies and in her room. She asks if her x-mas stuff is still there.

Night time is the worst for me. She has a lot of nightmares and groans a lot in her sleep as if she is in pain. That is hard. And I say all of this while also stressing that during the day, she really is a trooper. I mean how can she not be? There is the equivalent of gasoline running through her veins, and you wouldn't know it. I slept with her again last night, so you never sleep too well when you are with her, and every time I rolled over and looked at her beautiful bald head, it just reminded me that she is sick.

I guess when she didn't "look" like she had cancer; it wasn't as "real". I know that sounds odd and maybe I'm not explaining it right or putting the right words on it. Sometimes I still wish I could I go to sleep and when I wake up, it will all have been a horrible, horrible dream.

I make sure that I don't cry in front of her, and that if she is down in the dumps (which is usually only when she is tired), we try to act silly and get her mood up and take a nap as soon as we can. I know she is going to react and act based on our actions and moods, so I never want her to see one of my "bawls." But I also let her know that it's ok to be sad every now and then because this is a hard thing she is going through.

I hope today is a better day for me and an easy day on her. We go in to the hospital at 8 for her chemo, blood check, and to see Dr. Pui one last time before he goes to Europe. He said, "No worries, I am 7 hours difference, and can be here in no time." He really is an angel on her side. And he says for every one person cured at St. Jude, 1000 are cured around the world.

So that makes me happy to know that Lucy is helping to save 1000 other kids, and one day when she gets older, I want to make sure she realizes that.

Day 27, Jan 21, 2011 6:13am
I woke up freezing down here in Tennessee, and then checked the weather for my friends in Illinois! Yikes!! So sorry! Bet Taco was under the covers cuddled close to my mom last night!!!

Yesterday, we had our appointment around 8 am at the hospital. When we got there, Lucy wanted to take her hat off so she could show everybody her new haircut. Here I was bawling the night before about it, and she was so proud!! I love that little girl! We told her it may grow back a different color; she is hoping for pink!

And she has a very beautiful head. We have never seen it before! She came out with the thickest black hair when she was born. It stuck straight up; it never fell out, but just continued to grow, so this is our first time seeing her head. She is also quite proud that her and White look exactly alike!

We had a short hospital visit again yesterday. Basically, went in to see Pui, got some anti-nausea meds then the push of Ara-C chemo. Her blood counts are all going up, with the exception of platelets, which is normal. Chemo is killing those, and eventually will kill the other cells too. Her ANC was at 1200!! Good to see that it does in fact recover after chemo. Pui said it will drop by the 24th again to zero.

She also took a 4 hour nap yesterday! The longest since she has been here! Zach tried to sneak in the bed with me while she was sleeping, but she woke up telling him where he needed to be! Lol! It was nice to just lay next to each other, even for a few minutes.

We haven't slept in the same bed for 5 weeks and hardly have had time for a conversation longer than 5 minutes. She doesn't like it when we talk, so we text a lot! Yesterday, we were trying to talk about bills and such, and she kept interrupting, so Zach had to sternly tell her to wait her turn and not interrupt because mommy and daddy had things to discuss. She started crying. And it's the first time she has broken down without hair, and we looked at each other and felt horrible! Of course, I had to say, "Nice, make the bald cancer patient cry." Haha! We try to keep it "real" with her and follow discipline, but if you have ever disciplined a bald kid before, you know how tough that is!!

Lucy also felt good enough to play some games yesterday. We played Connect 4, but not the original way, her way, and she won every game! Then we threw down a game of UNO Moo! Lol, it was fun. Then I painted her fingers and toes.

The post from yesterday explained how I was worried that Lucy was losing her "spirit", and I had a good friend who herself has been battling breast cancer for many years send me a note. She said not to worry about the spirit, it's still there, it has just gone inside for now to fight the cancer, and that it will return. That meant the world to me to hear what Lucy must be feeling and thinking but can't put into words. I told my friend her and Lucy are going to kick cancers ass, and they are cancer BFFs! And I believe that. They are the two strongest women I know and that was before all this happened!! I always thought Lucy "fought like a girl"!

Yesterday as we were waiting, I had a lady approach me and ask if I had a child being treated here. And I said yes, she said my sister does too, and pointed to a lady. It was only their 2nd day here. She was a mess, like I was that day. She was asking questions, and then said her 10 year old doesn't know what he has, and she can't muster to tell him that it's cancer because to him cancer would be synonymous with death. Apparently, they had their parents, grandparents, and aunts and uncles all die from cancer. I felt bad for her, but I told her what everybody else told me. Childhood cancer (leukemia) is a very different bird than adult cancer. And that we decided to embrace the term, and all the others that go with it. To pretend it's something else, is to be afraid of it, to hit it head on is to defeat it.

I know where she is coming from; I had an aunt die of breast cancer when I was 18. It was a horrible death -- long and drawn out. She left two babies behind, and I know that killed her spirit. So cancer was always a very fearful term to me too. And not that it isn't scary and that I want to downplay it, but that was a long time ago in terms of research and science;

I see the proof in my friend I mentioned early. And it's a different cancer that Lucy is battling. Plus kids don't have a negative mind set unless you mold them to have one. I strongly believe that a positive outlook and attitude is half the fight. And I'm not alone in that. The human mind and spirit is so powerful that they are doing studies on how it affects the cure rate. That's why we are at the RMH and not in the hospital. That's why the protocol is designed to be "at home" treatment, and that's why the hospital is centered around catering to kids and keeping normal activities intertwined with cancer. I hope that mom sees that, and trusts her child to know the truth so he has the tools to fight this.

Day 27, Jan 21, 2011 7:42am
BTW, breakfast for our little Lucy: 2 eggs sandwiches with cheese, bag of Fritos, bowl of cheerios, 2 milks! Lol!

Day 28, Jan 22, 2011 6:09am

I must confess: the night shift security guard is spoiling me. He works Sunday through Friday and makes coffee at 5 am, and when I have to make it myself, I'm very disappointed!! I have a routine now, and I look forward to the coffee and silence every morning.

Lucy does her last dose of the Ara-C today until next Wednesday. This one seems to get her down in the dumps and have a significant amount of fatigue. She gets up to eat and go to the doctors and that is about it. The rest of time is spent in bed. And I think the boredom is driving her mad! She has games, activities, movies, and things to do, but I think she just wants to get out of bed and feel good doing it!

She got some awesome Beatle stuff yesterday (thank you Lola), and she has been playing with the playing cards. She loves them! Must have a card shark on our hands! And we put a poster on the front of our door of the Beatles, and every time we get back to our room, she giggles and says how handsome they are.

Then of course, the food really brightens her day. And she eats a lot!!! But the Prednisone that causes that will be done on Monday. We will slowly wean her off of that. Everyone tells us to let her eat whatever and whenever because there will come a time when she won't eat at all. She has gained a little over 5 lbs since we got here. I used to call her my "bag of bones" because she was always so damn skinny and had a hearty appetite. Now I call her my chunky monkey with her cheeks.

Anyhow, after today, she has no more IV chemo for 4 days! Yea! She takes one by mouth at night, and that's it. Then next week is the Ara-C again from Wednesday-Saturday. Then she is off of every single drug for 7 days!!!! Woo hoo!!! That's when we start phase two of our recovery plan!

Based on the light duty for the next two weeks, I'm going to go home to be with Jack. There are going to be times that both of us absolutely have to be up here, and now is not one of those times. And Jack needs his mama. I'm going to start working so we can get at least one income, and I'm going to get the house ready with a new air filtration system, new water system, new fridge, and massive cleaning duty!! If all goes as planned, she will get to come home around Feb 12 for 10 days!! Plus Zach and her do great. They get along better than her and I because she is my clone! We fight! Hahha!

Last night, we explained why I had to go home, and she was mad at me. Was mean to me all night. Lol! But when we asked her how she would feel if both of us were with Jack, and we explained, he needs one of us. She said she would be sad and understood. What 3-year-old do you know with that type of compassion and understanding? Plus daddy has all the nursing staff in his pocket. The two of them walk in a room and so much charisma is floating around, everybody wants to be around them.

They are a great team, and I am very fortunate to have a husband like that. He is truly amazing. He says he knows just how to pacify and deal with her because she is just like me, so he's had a lot of practice! And let me tell you, I am NOT an easy person to live with!! So practice he has definitely had!

I bought Lucy a bed rail last night so she can sleep in her own big bed all by herself! She loves it. That should help daddy get some sleep, too. And one of my friends sent her one of those eye covers for sleeping. She loves it! So now daddy won't have to go to bed when she does and turn off the lights. Hopefully that gives him an hour of "down time" at night. That had been one of the hardest adjustments on all of us. We get no alone time. And that serves true for Lucy as well. Since she had the bed rail, Zach and I were able to sleep together in the same bed. How nice that was. Of course, Lucy is right, he steals all the covers!!

I'm packed and ready to go and plan on leaving around 9 am. I haven't told Jack; I want to surprise him! Might even order a mama Teresa for dinner!! Yummo!!

Again, thank you to everybody for the continued support. We are very grateful. And we see that some people don't have an ounce of what we have. We feel very fortunate, even while treating Lucy with cancer. With a huge cheering section out there, we know we will defeat this "bump" in the road. Okay, more like a boulder!!

Day 29, Jan 23, 2011 7:22am
HOME! And I think that is all I need to say about that. The last time, I felt quite guilty about leaving Lu, but this time, I'm ok with it. Jack is in great need of some talking and one on one time. Plus I told him he had to clean his room this morning, and the fit that came from that was awesome! LOL! I plan on getting stuff ready these next two weeks for Lucy to come home. We are hoping for some time around Feb 12. So I have a lot to do, plus I plan on working these two weeks.

I am very, very, very, very fortunate to have a wonderful employer who has been nothing but overly supportive. I hear a lot of families who don't have even a fraction of what we have. I think it will be good for me to get in the groove of things because we are going to have to be traveling back and forth to Memphis for 3 years, and we still have bills to pay here, so at least one of us has to keep on the payroll. We are hoping that both of us can stay on there, but for now Zach is taking a little time off. While you are down there, there is no time to work. The constant care that Lucy needs consumes your day from the time she gets up to the time she goes to bed, and its normally from around 5 am to 12 am.

I have had people ask if they can come see Lucy when she does come home, and the answer is unfortunately "no". She will still have low counts, so unless they are up, we cannot risk it. If she gets sick or anything, they stop the protocol and have to wait for her to get better to resume it. And at this stage, we don't want to postpone anything. The 8 weeks of her 2nd phase of protocol (where she is home every other week) is important to make sure the cancer cells are not recreating. After we get rid of all of them (we are hoping they are ALL gone by Feb 8th), we have to make sure they stay away. It will be around April before she can have any visitors. And even then, it will depend on her numbers on a weekly basis.

Lucy and Daddy had fun last night. He was able to keep her out of the room and playing downstairs for 3 hours!!! Usually, she just goes down there to eat and then comes back to the room to lay down. He said she was "rowdy" last night. She had her last dose of Ara-C until next Wednesday, and she goes off Prednisone tomorrow. She was also de-accessed last night from her port. Which basically means her needle that is usually constantly in her port was taken out. She doesn't have to have it put back in until Monday, so tonight, she will get to take a real bath!!! Yea!!!

Also, since I am at home, Zach is going to give updates on this site from St. Jude, and I will give updates from home. So that is an extra special treat ;)

Also, we have a lot of videos we have been uploading to YouTube. If you sign on and go to subscriptions, you can subscribe to weberzach and webershawna and you can see what we upload.

If all goes as planned and I actually get to stay home for the two weeks, I plan on taking Jack to the benefit on the 5th in Lexington. I think it would be good for him to see how much people are thinking and praying for us and the support that people are giving. May help him to understand the gravity of the situation a little better, and I want to show our appreciation. Because we are still blown away by people's generosity. Plan for today: make a to-do list, clean the house, and start the to-do list. :)

Day 30, Jan 24, 2011 7:20am
Night time is definitely the worst. I had a very 'Debbie downer' moment last night. I think it was because I watched a movie that made me cry and that just exasperated the situation. Plus, when you are all alone and have time to actually sit down and think about what is going on, it drives you mad. Zach and I were talking last night and the worst things for us are her lack of energy and physical changes. She doesn't look, sound, or act like the Lucy we know. And the thing that bothers me the most: she

hasn't danced. That is her favorite thing to do.

Zach said she pretty much ate all day yesterday. Today is last day for Prednisone, so that should cease. I think she had something crazy like 2 things of mac n' cheese, 4 hotdogs, 2 pizzas, and countless Fritos. LOL!

Jack had a rough night too last night. He broke down crying telling me how much he misses Lucy. And then he keeps telling me he doesn't feel well and needs to go to the doctor. He has been complaining about his stomach hurting for some time, but he eats fine, and when I push on it, it's fine and not hurting. I wonder if its stress. I get a horrible stomach ache when I am stressed out, and I think the poor kid has my genes when it comes to stress.

I am going to call Dr. Marley today. Hell, after taking Lucy to the doctor for what we thought was strep throat and finding out it was leukemia, I will be taking the kids to the doctor for every little thing they have now! LOL! Paranoia at its best.

Plus Jack really likes Dr. Marley, so I think I can get him to talk to Jack about this, and I will trust his advice if he thinks I should have him see a counselor. This is affecting Jack more than Lucy sometimes. He is older and knows more about what is going on around him. And maybe he's just faking a stomach ache and wants to go to the doctor for attention. I mean he sees Lucy getting all kinds of attention from being at the doctor. The thing that Jack won't like is he may have to have extra immunization shots as well as flu shots. Since Lucy will be home in 3 weeks, he has to have them at least 2 weeks prior to coming into contact with her or she can "catch" the viruses. And he has to be treated a little bit different and with extra precautions since Lucy has no immune system. That is our worst fear when she comes home; Jack is still going to school and around all kinds of germs on a daily basis.

Well, I better get Jack ready for school, and then I'll call to check on Lu after her 9:30 appointment and run errands around here. Must say going from 40 degrees to "feels like" 19 is not pleasant.

Day 31, Jan 25, 2011 5:54am

We got some GREAT news yesterday for Lucy. All of her blood work is NORMAL!!!! First time EVER! Woo hoo!!!! So excited because it could mean wonderful, wonderful things. It could mean remission. That is what we are hoping for. We will find out around Feb 12 or so if it is, in fact, remission.

She also had a great afternoon with daddy. She was a little more energetic than before, but did have one "roid rage". Daddy was cooking her dinner and she insisted that he cook one for her baby "White", and he refused to waste food on the doll. She screamed for about 7 minutes straight.

Zach said other parents were coming over to offer assistance because it was so bad, and when he told them why she was mad, they had to laugh. They have kids on steroids too....so they understand. BUT...yesterday was her last day of steroids for at least 7 weeks! Woo hoo!! They are just taking her off of it and told Zach she may get the shakes for a few days as it works out of her system, but nothing major. So we shall see how her appetite does, and if we get any relief on her big belly and chubby cheeks.

Today, she gets a day off. No hospital visits or anything. Tomorrow she starts the Ara-C again, which seems to fatigue her pretty badly.

Zach posted some more videos on YouTube of her seeming "almost" normal. Today is the start of week 5 of induction. Last week of any medications; next week and the final week of induction she goes off everything.

Yesterday was a busy, busy day for me. I started doing all the research for our water and air filtration system. I am fortunate to have some help from my family, friends, and mainly my uncle yesterday. He ran all over trying to get some answers about our water.

Here is our dilemma: we live on a community well shared by about 80 households. The water is nasty; always has been. The people who own the houses do not own the well. Its privately own by some guy who is a real jerk. He treats it when he wants to. So we will never know if the water is treated and free from bacteria. We have never drank the water, and we will be doing bottled water for drinking and cooking, but we still have to worry about bathing. For normal, healthy people, it is no big deal. But for Lucy, it can be life threatening if her ANC is below 500 and she bathes in water that has bacteria. So what we are looking at is a "mini treatment plant" of sorts. This way we can ensure water coming in our house is treated and free from bacteria.

There are a lot of systems out there that *claim* they can remove these things, so finding one that actually can was a pain. I think we may have found a solution after searching and talking to experts yesterday. It should run us around $3000 to put the system in, now we just have to find space for the system!! Our tiny house will need some serious rearranging and overhaul :). We are still doing the research on air filter systems; we have found one that I think is going to work, and we have to ensure our ducts get cleaned. Our ducts are in the crawl space, so we also have to make sure they get sealed off so there is no moisture that can produce mold. I think we are going with a whole house HEPA and UV light filter. That is not going to be cheap either, but totally worth it. We can't bring Lucy home until we get these things done, so I am hoping to order the equipment today and schedule a date for install. I was exhausted and stressed to the max by time we got this done yesterday.

I also had to take Jack to the doctor. He had been complaining about a stomach ache and head ache, and I thought it was nerves, but definitely wanted Doc to confirm. He agreed. He said the stress of what is happening to him and that things are different are tearing Jack up. He also said the mind of a 5 year old is fantasy and self-centered, so he is probably blaming himself that this happened.

And doc hit it right on the nose. Jack said that he was Lucy's big brother and that he was supposed to take care of her and protect her, and he couldn't do that, and didn't do that because she got sick. We decided that counseling would be best for him. He seemed pretty excited about being able to talk to somebody about his feelings and having the attention focused on him. He also had to get a flu shot...he was not happy. Bet he doesn't ask to go to the doc for a long time.

I also did some work yesterday. It was nice to merge with the real world for a while. It's going to be busy and hectic, but to turn your mind onto something else was very nice. I am also going to go to lunch today with some dear, dear co-workers, and I am super stoked to see them. They have always helped me ground myself, so should be good therapy.

All in all, yesterday was busy, but it was a fantastic day. And I take things day by day now, so yesterday was a success. Got a lot of research done, stress eliminated, Lucy had a great day, Jack was the happiest I had seen or heard from him in weeks. At the end of the day, we talked on the phone to daddy and Lucy. Jack was so excited and didn't want her to hang up. They talked to each other for quite some time. It was sweet. Although our family is 500 miles apart, for a moment last night, it was as if the four of us were all together again. I slept like a baby.

Day 32, Jan 26, 2011 6:53am
Good morning Friends and Family. You know I have been home since Saturday evening, and it feels like FOREVER without Zach and Lucy.

When I was in Memphis, it felt the same way without Jack. Guess I just can't be pleased!! Something Zach says about me often. In one way, I am excited that I still have another week here, and on the other hand, I am ready to rush back to Memphis. Even thinking how I could manage to go back early! LOL! But with all the things that need to be done to the house, I know that is not possible.

Yesterday, I got our water service started for cooking and drinking water, finally decided upon a whole house water filtration for bathing, received our new water heater, and did some other household errands.

It felt good to accomplish some things. I also worked a bit yesterday and went to lunch with some co-workers. That was nice, to have a dose of reality. For a moment, life seemed "normal". Even last night cooking in my own kitchen felt nice. Although, I have to admit, I forgot where some things were stored. I don't know why; I do all the cooking here, so I have no idea why I can't find things.

Lucy and daddy had the whole day off, so no hospital visits. She had a few fits from coming off the steroids, nothing major, and she is ordering daddy around. He did say her appetite seemed to lessen a bit. I think she is bored, but doesn't feel good enough to really get up and play, so every few minutes she asks daddy to get something or do something for her. I will be excited when she starts dancing again.

She starts her ARA-C doses again today. She will get those Wednesday-Saturday, along with finishing up the oral chemo she gets at night by Monday. Then starting Tuesday she is OFF everything!!! Woo hoo!! That will be a true test when we get her blood work. To see how her body does with no chemo in it in regards to the cancer cells. Another major milestone.

Today, I plan doing some de-cluttering, closet cleaning, and making some trips to Goodwill. We needed to do this BEFORE the cancer, and I was a procrastinator. So nothing like giving me a reason to get something done that needed to be done anyhow! I asked Zach to post on here today because he can give a better account of how Lubelle is doing. Plus, he tells the stories better and is pretty darn funny about her fits and rages. I also wanted to let folks know that the benefit team is pre-selling tickets for Lucy's benefit on Feb 5th.

Tickets are $15 for adults and there is a suggested donation for children. You can buy tickets at Choice Cuts in Colfax, Long Branch in Cooksville, Kemps and Shake Shack in Lexington, and Coconut Louie's in Bloomington. You can also buy at the door the day of the benefit. Jack and I plan on attending to thank our supporters in person. I am amazed at the generosity of people and very humbled.

Day 32, Jan 26, 2011 10:41pm
Hello from Memphis,
I'm Zach. I haven't posted on here before, but since I'm staying down here, it just makes sense I do an update. When Lucy first started showing signs of cancer, it was bruises. I was the one that would say: "Quit being so darned clumsy, and go rub some dirt on it". After receiving several medical opinions, I've found out that rubbing dirt on it does not really cure cancer. Go figure.

Lucy is doing well. Her numbers are dropping lower again. Which is good. I was a little concerned about how "well" her numbers looked on Monday, but today I see they are falling. That's actually a good thing, I think. Since she did a week of ARA-C, all her fast growing cells should be dying (that includes the immune system, hair cells, and cancer cells). Since I see the numbers dropping, it tells me that something is in there killing off stuff (good and bad stuff). Dr. Pui said to expect her ANC to be 0 by the 25th. I think we were at 600 today, so we never totally made it to 0. Today she started her 2nd week of ARA-C. I believe that will drop her counts very low. It's good, since that will kill the cancer, but it really makes you nervous about infection and illnesses.

Yesterday was her first day without steroids. She laid in bed pretty much all day. I think it's like going from drinking a pot of coffee 3 times a day to nothing. Since she wasn't getting her "fix", she just didn't have the energy to do much more than lay in bed and watch movies. You can tell she gets bored. When she's bored, she starts messing with me. She'll throw a pillow on the floor and ask me to pick it up. Or she'll ask me to turn off some random light. She likes to know she has some control even though she's in bed. She's also just plain bored.

I keep her spirits up the best I can. I tell everyone that I left my marbles in Illinois, so I just act like a fool down here. It keeps

Lucy entertained. It's not rare that I walk around pretending I'm a chicken or some other farm animal. People laugh, the kids laugh, and it keeps Lucy entertained. I pretend I'm on vacation in Disney World; it's helping me keep a good attitude, and hold things together.

Today was an early day. I was up at 5:30 to start getting ready. I had Lucy up at 6, and she was ANGRY! She did not want to be awake today. We made our 7:45 appointment for blood draws. Then we waited. About an hour and fifteen minutes later we were called for the 2nd appointment. During that time, she laid against my chest and didn't complain a bit. She really wants to feel better, and doesn't mind the hospital at all. During our second appointment we changed buddy's blanket, and she was very calm. I was very proud of her. Usually she cries, but not today. She sat back and instructed the nurse on the proper techniques.

Next, it was off the medicine room for chemo. All the nurses gather around for that. Every time she comes in, the nurses come by to talk. They say Lucy is sooo cute and funny and talks so well. But I know they all just want to see me! Hahahaha!

In the medicine room, they told us that Dick's Sporting Goods was visiting today, and giving away a free pair of crocs to all the patients. So I carried Lucy over to the next building to check it out. We had to sign some type of consent form, so they could video tape her getting new shoes. I think they plan on using it for some type of promotional video for Dick's Sporting Goods. So I hammed it up pretty good. I took baby White out of the back pack and put on a pair of size 12 men's shoes on her and made her walk around. Lucy was belly laughing so loud.

Lunch was next. Her appetite is a fraction of what it was during the steroids. She had just 5 chicken nuggets. Before, 5 chicken nuggets would have been a pre-appetizer, or a post-dessert snack. They say the loss of appetite is normal, and her body has plenty of calories stored up. She just needs to stay hydrated.

After lunch and waiting for the shuttle, we finally made it "home". Lucy walked in the door, turned out the lights, and said, "Lay down; it's nap time." It was so funny, because she said it in such a stern voice.

She laid in bed and didn't want to do anything until the mail came. Then she really perked up. My Uncle Denny and Aunt Cheryl had sent a little kit with shoe strings and wooden beads to make bracelets and necklaces. She LOVED it. She played with that all night. We even made a necklace for White.

We also got a package from my mom's first cousin, Deb Weber. It's overwhelming to see the support you get from all over the country. That's one of the strangest parts of all this.

Since this is my first post, I'll keep going... I've got a lot to say.

Staying at the Ronald McDonald house is weird. I love that we have a place to stay, but it's weird. The staff is amazing. It takes some special people to keep all this together. I'll do a video tomorrow of a tour. It's a pretty big place. The weird parts are sharing kitchens and whatnot. But the worst part is seeing all the other kids with cancer.

And Lucy has "good" cancer. Many aren't that lucky. It's very sad so see these kids battle for their health. Some are doing better, some aren't. You see parents crying out of sight. You hear people on the phone talking about finances, health, bad test results, and good ones too. It's a jacked up place to live. The night time is the worst. That's when your guard is down. You don't have to be goofy and happy anymore. You aren't preoccupied with taking care of a cancer patient (which is like caring for a newborn that can talk). The depression sets in at night. The kids are all in bed, the parents are all out talking amongst themselves about what to do for their family, and worrying about how the next day will go. For me, it's sleep. I don't sleep well here. I stare at the ceiling a lot. Lucy has nightmares and tends to yell and scream in her sleep, so that keeps me up.

As I was writing this, a woman that we've made friends with ran out of her room screaming bloody murder for help. I ran over, but security was there already. Her son was not responding, and the ambulance is here now to take him to the hospital (I call it the big house).

So that's the depressing part. The great part is the people and the hospital. Our nurses, Justine, Regina and Martha, are amazing people. I bombard them with questions all the time. I harass them about drinking in their little lounge room. I accuse them of sneaking pills from the pharmacy, and they continue to put up with my goofball attitude day in and day out.

Dr. Pui is, well, Dr. Pui. He's great with the kids. I'm still trying to break him though. He has a sense of humor buried deep down inside, and there's been a couple times I've dug it up. He returns from a week absence tomorrow, so it'll be good to hear his thoughts on our progress.

Another great part of being here is Lucy. She's amazing. She puts up with so much crap, and rarely complains. She never complains about chemo, doctors, or the hospital. She only throws fits over things that matter, like candy, bedtime, and TV.

Tomorrow will be another early day and much like all the days before. I continue to cluck like a chicken, ask random people for money or beer, and of course, take care of Lucy. I didn't mean to be depressing on my first post, just telling it like it is.

Go rub some dirt on it; you'll be fine.

Day 33, Jan 27, 2011 7:02am
Today is day 31 of Lucy's treatment plan. Hard to believe we have only been at it for 31 days! Just a month? Really? I was saying that this time at home was going by slow, but yesterday after I made my to-do list and started on tasks, I felt rushed and pressured. I thought.. how am I going to get all this stuff done by time I leave to go back to Memphis on Feb 7th?

Then I just broke things down into little chunks and prioritized them. I think I can do it; just be super busy. Which is actually fine by me. When I'm not busy, my mind is idle, and I start to think... thinking is NOT good.

I want to say how proud I am of my husband for his post last night. He's not one to like to write, and I think he did a fantastic job. He made me laugh and cry and miss him and Lubelle to pieces. We did get to video chat last night, and Lucy looked good! She looked happy and not tired. When Jack saw her, he started crying. He misses her so much. I can't wait to have her home and them two fighting again.

Last night, after Jack had gone to bed, I watched a movie, and missed Zach even more than ever. It was a funny, stupid movie. And what I love about those movies more than anything is his laugh. I miss his laugh. He and I usually laugh at things that others would think were stupid. And there were a lot of those parts.

I was feeling good last night, feeling like we had this cancer thing beat even though we are still only into the beginning of treatment. I thought this is hard, but we are doing just fine. Then, I got a text from Zach that the ambulance was there, and my heart sank. A dose of reality to ensure we weren't getting too comfortable! The little boy that was taken out had problems breathing and was unresponsive. I told Zach to check Lucy all night! He laughed and said "I'm already taking her temperature". So we both had the same idea. The boy did come to finally after getting oxygen. Not sure why he couldn't breathe; apparently he hasn't been able to for a few days. Asthma, we think.

Yesterday, I got a lot accomplished. I got our drinking water delivered and set up, I scheduled the duct cleaning for next Monday, found a new refrigerator I like (now I have to go look in person and try to strike a deal), and cleaned out all the closets and the kitchen cabinets. I cloroxed everything!!! Granted, it looks like the rest of my house threw up in my living room and on my counters!! LOL! I have to find space for some things and take other things to consignment shops and probably a trip to Goodwill. I had a friend come pick up 5 bags of clothes, blankets, etc yesterday and took them there for me, which was awesome and a huge time saver!!!

I also got a lot of our bills figured out and called companies to see where we could get some breaks, switch over some billing plans, etc. And then I had to get Zach's stuff figured out since he won't be pulling a paycheck, and he has stuff like life insurance that comes directly out of his pay. Got our garbage service started back up, which is much needed, and they will have a big load this week! They were so kind and told us the next 3 months were free. People have kind hearts.

I also actually ordered our water treatment plant, at least half of it! LOL! We just need to more pieces for it. And it's basically going to take up our entire mud room, so we will have to put our washer and dryer in the garage, which means we will have to heat that. So I still have that to order, but in our list of priorities that isn't high on the list, so first things first.

I also did some more work-work yesterday. Starting to jump in and get in the groove. I am planning on going into the office today and tomorrow to get some things I need from my desk and talk to some of my folks. I'm nervous about that. I am not sure if I am ready to be bombarded with people. I may sneak in quietly and close my office door. Anybody that knows me, knows that is NOT like me! I am a VERY social being, so much so, I think one of my co-workers, Jim, wishes I would just give my mouth a rest for a few minutes. I'm getting my hair cut this morning. Thought I better get one in for the next 6 months. :)

Day 34, Jan 28, 2011 6:11am
Definitely appreciate being home, but I miss the security guard. I have to make my own coffee at home. Boo! Zach used to make it every morning for me, so again, spoiled!

Yesterday was such a busy day, I feel like it flew right by. I was telling Zach that when I look at all the things that need to be done, it feels like I don't have enough time, but when I see how long it is until I get to see him and Lubelle, it seems like FOREVER! Amazing how much perspective can help you change your mind set about a situation. I mean here I have the SAME situation, but looking at it two different ways changes my mindset and attitude completely! I had a wonderful Dale Carnegie instructor who said that we have control over one thing in this world, and this is our mind. People can't tell us how to think about something; we have a choice about how we are going to "show up" for the day. And I thought I knew how to do that, but I didn't, until now. I also have a new perspective about Cancer.

I mentioned before about the lady who didn't want to tell her son what it was he had because cancer was always synonymous with death? Well, I have to say before this event, I was a little on that fence. I mean I have seen what cancer has done to several family members, but then again, I have seen what my friend has done to cancer. And now that Lucy has it, I have decided to jump the fence completely and not ever think cancer is synonymous with anything. It's a thing that has happened and continues to happen to people, and it sucks and its horrible, but it doesn't define anything except that we have to take time out of the next 3 years of our lives to get rid of it. That's it. I'm giving it no more power than it deserves.
Which BTW, I don't know if my mindset would be this great given the situation if I hadn't taken that Dale Carnegie class last year. See, everything does happen for a reason. Little did I know how much I would be pulling from that class in regards to my personal life considering the class is offered by and paid for by my employer. Oh, ok, and Xanax has helped me too! Ha! Got to give credit where credit is due.

Yesterday, I went into work. I was nervous about seeing people, but it was good. It was ok to talk about things, and I didn't get all emotional like I was afraid I would. And I know given the circumstances, it would be perfectly ok to be emotional, but I didn't want to do that there. It was nice to hear about people following the journal and all of their support. And that is so funny… Sometimes, I forget others read this. This has been so therapeutic for me. I've never been one for journaling because I always felt odd, like I was talking to myself, but this is actually really comforting. And I love to read the guest book and see how many people are cheering for Lucy. I plan on printing this out and saving it for her. I want her to see the kindness in the world when she gets older, and read the triumphs and struggles she went through.

And let's talk about that little 3 year old!! I love her so much, and she is quite possibly the strongest person I have ever met and she doesn't even understand what that means yet! As Zach mentioned, she never complains about the hospital; she wants to get better. She is doing so good now with her medicine and buddy changes. She has meltdowns and fits, but what three year old doesn't? She is bored. And I can't blame her. She is accustomed to going to daycare, being social around other children, and she misses her best friend, Cole. She is used to going to ballet once a week, and then playing with Jack the rest of the week. And now she gets stuck in a shoe box with daddy! Ha! I talked to her yesterday and asked if she was having a good day or a rough day. She said "Mommy, I'm having a rough day. Daddy won't let me watch Superman 1; he wants to watch Superman 2". HAHAHA, classic Lucy, telling on daddy. She is in love with Superman like she is the Beatles! She thinks he is handsome.

Lucy has always been such a free spirit, and people are drawn to her charisma. Even as a baby, people were drawn to her, although I think it was her hair! She really has no idea what this ordeal means except that she has to get rid of the cancer bugs so she can come home. She has to fight them and take her medicine like a big girl, and that is what she is doing. I was looking at x-mas pictures and thinking "Wow, she was so sick on x-mas day, and we had no clue". She was still spunky and throwing fits! Ha! And it was still a very magical day for her. I was sad when I looked at those photos, then it occurred to me, we got to have x-mas at home. And she got that "normalcy", as did Jack, so we are fortunate.

Yesterday, I finished cleaning the kitchen inside and out. And started on the bathroom. We have a very tiny house, and normally it wouldn't take so long, but I'm scrubbing everything! And I took garbage to the curb, I think something crazy like 12 bags. If we haven't used it in 6 months, then I tossed it. I separated what can go to Goodwill, and what just shouldn't :). Zach was proud... I never take out the garbage! LOL!

I'm also the worst mommy ever, according to Jack. :). He said before Memphis, we didn't have these rules. He must have forgotten because I have changed no rules, just enforced them! He has to (gasp) get dressed for school before he's allowed to watch TV, and he has to (gasp) eat dinner at the table with me. And heaven forbid if he has to go to bed on time. I'm the worst mommy ever and this is the worst day ever. I hear that every day at some point, which just means I'm doing my job correctly.

Today promises to be another long day. I am going into work again this morning, then running errands this afternoon before getting home when Jack gets off the bus. Then tonight, cleaning again. I think I'll tackle Lucy's room and organize everything. I'm not doing floors, walls, etc. yet; I'm going to wait until the duct cleaning is done because it will kick up tons of dirt anyhow. Then tomorrow I HAVE to do the laundry room. I have to find space for everything that is in there now so we can put the water treatment plant in there. And in order to find room for that stuff, I may have to clean the garage out. Which is NOT pretty!

It's our storage area basically since our house is so small. And we aren't master organizers; we throw stuff in there. So trying to put that off to the last thing I do.

Lucy and daddy have a hospital trip today to get blood work, see the nurse, and get her daily dose of ARA-C. Her numbers should be bottomed out soon. Which is totally normal. We want to see them bottomed out, actually. Just means the chemo is doing its nasty little job.

Day 35, Jan 29, 2011 7:01am
I think Zach is also secretly in love with the security guard. He

just texted me "mornin". Then a few minutes later, he texted me and said, "Ugh, no coffee". So I do believe he understands the importance of the early morning coffee already made. The security guard is off Saturday and Sunday. So it's every coffee drinker for himself!

I think I did more yesterday than I have done in a long time, and that's a sad statement to make because I'm talking even before the cancer! :) I actually got to do my hair, wear makeup, and wear dress clothes with heels!!!

It felt nice to do more than just brush my teeth. I went into work for the morning, then I ran errands in the afternoon for about 2 hours, then last night, I had some friends come over and help me clean Lucy's room. We got it all organized and weaned out some of her toys. I hope she doesn't notice! I also went through a ton of papers and mail that has been accumulating. We got our bill from when we were at St. Francis for one day. Total amount was just over $17,000. And that doesn't include the labs! That was the room and board type of expense. YIKES!! I know medical is expensive, but $17,000!!! That's like a car! And then we got separate bills from radiology and pathology for around $800, and we still have the doctor bills to come. Thank goodness it was the end of the year and we had already met our deductible. Because if we hadn't, we would be paying over $7000. Our portion is still close to $1000 so far. And that was just one day.

I am so thankful for St. Jude. We don't pay out-of-pocket expenses or co-pays or even prescriptions while we are down there. When we come back home, we will be responsible for whatever we have, but that shouldn't be anywhere near $17,000! And I guess I shouldn't just thank St. Jude, but everybody that donates there. You make it possible for parents to treat their children and not worry about "how to pay for it". I think our total for St. Jude by day 17 is estimated at something crazy in the million dollar range or close to it. I would also like to take this time to thank Mr. Obama for doing away with lifetime limits. For all you haters of the president, I for one, am truly thankful for that law change. Ok, so enough politics and money..... :)

I got to talk to Zach on the phone last night after the kids went to bed for something crazy like an hour and 1/2. Anybody that knows my husband knows that is NOT like him. He hates to talk on the phone. It was nice, and it was probably the first real conversation we have had in 6 weeks. We discussed Lucy, Jack, the bills, and then we talked about how we felt about this whole situation. He gave me updates on the other families we met down there and how the children are doing. And it's odd because I can honestly say that we don't just talk about beating this and just saying the words, we both truly feel that this is definitely an obstacle, but other than that, it's our new normal. I didn't think I would ever get used to our new normal like the nurses said we would, but we have.

And Lucy is amazing to both of us. Everybody posts about how strong she is, and you know, she truly is strong. She is dealing with this better than most adults I know would. She really wants to come home, but she told daddy last night, I can come home after we beat the cancer bugs, right? He said yes. She said well, I have two cancer bugs left. And she is adamant that is all that is left! 2! And who knows! She could be totally right. We think there is Zero, though ;)

Zach also said she had a burst of energy last night. She got up and was running!! RUNNING! around the room. She hasn't ran since we have been there. She was pretending to be superman. Today is her last dose of ARA-C. Then two more days on the oral chemo she gets at night. Then she is off of everything for a whole week!

She is also being weaned off the Labetol that she takes for her high BP. The Prednisone caused the high BP, and she hasn't take that since Monday, so her BP is leveling out just fine. That will leave her on just one medicine, and that may get to go to. The Gabapenton is what she takes for neuropathy pain caused by one of the chemos. It causes nerve pain in her jaw, legs, feet, and hands. But, after seeing her running last night, Zach said he was going to ask if she can come off of it.

He was also explaining to me last night about the side effects of the high dose Methotrexate she will get next. Most common: vomiting. I hate to see her vomit. She hasn't done too bad with the others, and she gets the Zofran to help with that, but the nurses say that with this chemo, sometimes the Zofran doesn't even help. So basically she will get this chemo and have to be admitted for a few days. We aren't sure when she will get it; it will depend on a few factors with her blood work. So it could be Feb 8th or it could be sooner or later. I'm hoping it's not sooner just because I'm not scheduled to go back down to Memphis until the 6th or 7th.

Then she will get released from inpatient care after she clears the chemo, and her blood work numbers recover to a certain level. At that time, we get to drive her home. I'm nervous and excited about that drive! Nervous because we aren't close to our home base of St. Jude, and excited because I can't wait for her to be home. Of course, it's only for about 10 days, but a visit will be nice. I'm already dreading the drive back to Memphis for her next treatment. She's not going to be happy about being home and then leaving again, and I don't blame her.

Then I guess the schedule and treatment isn't as cut and dry as I thought. I thought we would be going back every other week for the high dose Methotrexate, but really its dependent on her body and how quickly her numbers recover before she can get the chemo, and again before she can be released to come home-home. So it could very well take a lot longer than 8 weeks. And the logistics of that will be rough. 24 hour, around the clock parent is needed when we are inpatient, and that is rough on one parent, so we both would like to be there for these treatments, but then Jack is home, so we will play it by ear on how this works out. And they say that every child reacts differently to this chemo, and they even react different each time they get it. So our first dose may have no effects or complications, and our last one could have a lot.

The other thing I'm a bit nervous about is Jack has a cold :(. I hope that is all it is. He has a stuffy/running nose and a little cough.

I've been using hand sanitizer like I should buy stock in it. And been kissing his forehead, etc. If I get sick, I can't go back down to Memphis until I'm better, and a cold can last WEEKS!! I'm taking my vitamins and cloroxing everything... we shall see if that helps. But you know, we are going to have to learn how to live with that because Jack will get colds and other things from school, and we can't quarantine him or Lucy from each other. So we are going to install some of those wall pump sanitizers in our house! Hahahah ok, so maybe not, but its crossed our minds. BTW, Lucy calls it "hanitizer". Hehehehe!

Plans for today: clean Jack's room, clean and organize bathroom, and start cleaning and organizing our closet. And then the only thing I will have left is the laundry room and garage! Woo hoo! Of course I haven't scrubbed walls and floors or anything because it would be pointless. We are getting our ducts cleaned on Monday, and that should kick up quite a bit of nastiness. Thank goodness for all wood floors!! Those should be easy to clean.

Daddy and Lucy are going into the hospital for her last dose of chemo, then they get tomorrow off. I think cabin fever is setting in for both of them. Since her numbers are crashing, she really can't leave the room that often except to eat, which BTW, her appetite is less than half of what it was! which is totally normal, so we shall see if that potbelly starts to go down.

Day 36, Jan 30, 2011 7:22am
I got to video chat with Lucy last night, and she looks good. Even looks a little less chubby. She also looks BORED! Zach said they are getting cabin fever bad. She is throwing some pretty massive fits for him over stupid stuff. She brushed her teeth about 6 times yesterday (or more), changed her clothes at least 3 times, would watch 5 minutes of a video and be ready to put in a new one. And yesterday in Memphis, it was something crazy like 69 degrees, and she couldn't even go outside to enjoy it. While we don't know her counts and numbers, she should be bottomed out to zero by now. So taking no risks of her getting sick.

Tuesday marks her last week of induction. Last night, we made silly faces and threw hugs and kisses to each other. We sang some Beatles' songs and it was good to see her giggle. Since her cheeks are going down a little bit, I can see "my Lucy" again in her eyes. And her voice seems to be going back to normal. It was high pitch and squeaky. I was joking with her about her hair. I kept asking her "What happened to all your hair?? Where did go?" She said "mommy, we chaved it (shaved), remember?" and then she would giggle.

And Zach looks good... too good! LOL! What is it about men? He has lost so much weight! He is about at the same weight he was when we met 7 years ago. WTH? Here I am eating weight watchers and running around cleaning and running errands, and I think I lost 7 lbs. So not fair! He got me Zumba for the Wii for x-mas, so I guess I better open the package. Before I know it, he will weigh less than me, and that just isn't right! Hahaha!

But while he looks good, he is bored to tears too. He is constantly at Lucy's beck and call, can't really have a "break" being the only parent there. He says it's like having a newborn baby again who commands all sorts of attention, and is helpless, only this time around, it's a 3 year old who can talk, throw fits, and WANTS to exhibit any form of independence she can. So it's totally like a new born baby mixed with a teenager! I totally agree with that assessment. 8 more days and I'll be there to relieve him. Yikes! Only 8 more days to get everything done.

Jack went to stay all night with Aunt Deanna last night, and he had a BLAST! He got to play with her granddaughter, Brooklyn, who is a year old. He really loved that. I think he misses Lucy, so playing with a younger girl was fun for him. I got the house to myself and had big plans for cleaning his room while he was gone. Yeah, that didn't happen. I sat on the couch with Taco and didn't move! It was nice. I felt a little guilty having some down time, when Zach has had no down time. I'm sure we will all get our turn though. We have three years of this. I am going to ask him to do another post today. I like his analogies, and he can give a better account of Lucy and how she is doing.

My son is now home and he too is commanding my attention like a toddler! HA! That is the one thing I have noticed. My 5 year old, who NEVER needed me, all of sudden wants me to do everything with him. Now I remember why we had Lucy! To entertain Jack and so they could babysit each other! Ha! :)

Day 37, Jan 31, 2011 6:24am
I got smart last night. Made my coffee and set the timer. So my coffee was all ready for me when I woke up! It did get me thinking since I often talk of the security guard… I am going to get his name when I go back down to Memphis and make sure I get him a little something to show how much his small gesture really starts my day in the right direction.

I asked Zach to journal last night, and he said he would today. He said if he wrote anything last night, it would definitely be a 'Debbie downer' moment. He found out why that little boy down the hall had to go to the hospital, and it was tearing him up.

We have talked to that family the entire time we were down there, and we had no idea that, in November, the doctors gave him 6 months to live. He has a rare form of cancer in his lymph nodes. They are sending the family home this week. That is never good. When they just stop treatments and send you home, it's for quality of life. And I cannot imagine that scenario with your child. Then Zach said another family moved into the house whose child has a rare liver cancer. So that is pretty much how things work at the RMH. It's awesome and provides you a place to stay close to your doctors, but then you also know that a couple of rooms down, another child may not have been as fortunate as yours to have the "good" cancer. And then you hate to see when one of the children you have gotten to know has to go inpatient. I ask Zach every night about each one and if they have been released to the RMH yet. You find yourself sitting on pins and needles for the other families. It's a weird environment to live in, and definitely a bond you create with others that is like no other I have ever experienced in my life.

Ok, so now I am going to totally out some of the employees of the

RMH (and I know they read this); they SPOIL my daughter to no end!! LOL!! She was throwing a fit, and got picked up by Debbie, one of the managers and she loved on her, and gave her candy. HAHAHA! They are big Lucy Fans, and we appreciate it! So much so, I better put a plug in for their big fund raiser coming up!

February is the big fund raiser that really gives them a lot of the money they need to run the house, and let families like us stay for FREE!! And they provide everything we need, and then some, to live comfortably.

Yesterday, I had a bit of a meltdown. I was becoming so overwhelmed by everything that needs to be done. I felt like things weren't moving fast enough and was worried that they wouldn't be complete by time I go back down to Memphis. I bawled for about 20 minutes, and that seemed to help. I took a deep breath and said "one thing at a time". And that helped too. Jack came over and patted my back, and said "It's going to be ok, Mom". He's such a sweet, caring boy.

I kicked it into high gear and the only thing left to organize here is the laundry room and Jack's room. After we get the air system installed, I'll start the scrub down. I'm also going to order the other piece we need for the water system. The stressful part about that is: its winter and damn cold. Hard to put in a system that requires draining, etc. Then we are getting all that damn snow this week! UGH! Which, BTW, will be done by Thursday, and being Illinois, will be clear by Saturday for the benefit. I know it will be.

Zach posted 5 more videos on YouTube of Lucy. They are pretty funny. So if you haven't seen them, subscribe to weberzach to see them. Lucy definitely has more energy and is turning back into her old self, even if just for a while. She is also not eating as much. She had a toaster strudel yesterday and drank 3-4 cartons of milk and that was it. The doctor said that was fine and normal; she has fat stored up!

Today, Lucy gets a blood draw to check her numbers, and that's it.

Today is also the last dose for her 6TG chemo she takes my mouth every night. So for the rest of the week, she has no more chemo! Then sometime next week, we get another bone aspiration to see if her leukemia is in remission. Send her all the positive thoughts and prayers you can!! We are hoping for remission!!!

Jack's cold is hopefully going to just stay a bad cold, and we have been sanitizing everything. I don't even kiss him anywhere near the face. Zach told him to go rub some dirt on it. Apparently, he knows it can't cure cancer, but still thinks it's a cure for all other ailments......

Day 37, Jan 31, 2011 9:15pm
Greetings from Memphis; this is Zach posting again... Today we were in the clinic for blood tests and regular vitals. Lucy has been taken off all meds but one. No more "Ticker" medicine, no more pain meds, and no more chemo for the moment. The idea here is to see what her body does, and how it responds. Her numbers are dropping, and she's back in the "Danger Zone" for infection. That was completely expected due to the 2 weeks of ARA-C. Her ANC is 400. They aren't sure if it's on its way down, or up at the moment.

We have tomorrow "off", but there's really no "off" day here. We just don't have to go to the hospital. Wednesday, we return to clinic to see blood tests. If they are on the way up, she will likely start her next phase on Friday. Otherwise, we will start on Monday. Her procedure will be another spinal, and MRD (which will tells us how much cancer is left), and start the high dose Methotrexate. She will be admitted into the hospital during that chemo treatment and will stay there until the chemo is flushed from her system and her numbers recover. At that point, we would be allowed to go home. So I'm still shooting to be home by Valentine's day.

If on Wednesday her numbers are lower, she will be put back on the preventative antibiotics. Those are the 3 hours of IV "medicine balls" and oral Cipro.

In terms of Lucy herself.... She's very wishy-washy. She may be happy and laughing one moment, then screaming on the floor the next. Cabin fever is getting to her, and she's tired of watching movies. We have some other toys to help keep her occupied, but she mostly likes to lay in bed and order me around.

Shawna has been hard at work, fixing the water situation at home and getting everything prepared. There's a lot to do, and she's doing a great job getting it all together. She'll be a licensed general contractor by the time this is all over. (Love you babe, you rock!)

Here at the Ronald McDonald house, Lucy continues to be spoiled by the staff up front. They are on her like white on rice. As noted in Shawna's earlier post, we are one of the lucky ones here. Since I've been staying here, I've seen a handful of kids that go home to live in peace until the inevitable happens. I don't understand how those parents are able to keep it together and walk the halls and live day-to-day. Often people break down, and start uncontrollably sobbing.

On the bright side, I did see another family as they received their results for the day 15 MRD. They have B cell ALL too. They came in at 0.009% which is amazing for day 15. They continue like everyone else, but they have the comfort of knowing that there are only a few cancer cells left in their child's body. The mother was screaming, jumping, and it was pretty exciting to see.

Like I said, we have tomorrow off. I plan on cleaning the room from top to bottom again. I see some dust bunnies under the bed, and I think they need to die.

I'll try to make more videos and take more pictures. It's important that my whole family can remember this far down the road. Especially when I'm old, and can't take care of myself. I'll be expecting my kids to mix butt paste and slop it on my ass every time I have to make poops. I think the videos and pictures will help guilt them into keeping me out of a nursing home. HAHA.

It'll also be good ammunition for when Lucy is a teenager, saying how little we do for her. :)

I miss my son. I miss my wife. I miss my home. But I wouldn't change any of this. It seems like boot camp sometimes, but worth every second. In the end, when Lucy is cured, my family's reward will be just that... Family.

On a side note... I know it's Monday because there was coffee made this morning. The last show I watched on cable was "A Christmas Story" on TBS. I've lost 14 pounds. I've learned to keep calm; I've learned a good deal of discipline. And I REALLY, REALLY would like a beer.

That's all for now folks. Go rub some dirt on it; you'll be fine.

Feb 1, 2011 7:31am

Today, we get a snow day back here at home!! Yea!! Jack had no idea what a snow day was; this is his first. So he was like "Yea, so?" I said, "Do you know the importance of a snow day, son?" I had to explain why this was so awesome. I let him stay up a little late last night, and then when he woke up this morning, he said "We aren't snowed in; it looks fine". HAHAHAHA! It wouldn't have mattered if we were snowed in or not, I would have been stuck at home cleaning for the rest of the week anyhow!

Yesterday I got Jack's room done and started on the laundry room. Jack's room took FOREVER!! Mainly because he just had a lot of junk in drawers and his toys were not all in one place. I spent at least a good portion of time using Goo Gone and a Pampered Chef scraper to remove stickers from his floor!! I have to do Lucy's room too. They love their stickers; I do not so much. :) Stamps too. They like to sneak and stamp the walls from time to time. Oh well...it's just paint and can be redone.

The ducts got cleaned yesterday. That is a huge relief to me. We ordered our filters, and they said since our house is small that is really all we need... some good filters. So that saves us about $1500. Woo hoo!! Cuz I will take that money and buy a new fridge, which I did last night. Ours leaks water, and that's normal for most fridges to do that a little, but ours creates mold at the bottom. Before, I would clean it out on a regular basis and it wouldn't get bad or super nasty, but now, we can't even risk it.

Uncle Denny came over yesterday and was a life saver. He took down some cabinets so I could get a new fridge in and not have to worry about the height, he got salt for our water softener, and he worked on getting our sump pump to drain so it's not passing through the septic tank. That will be one challenge with our new water system; it will be draining a lot of water, so we couldn't have it pass through the septic or it could cause major issues. I am VERY thankful for his help.

My mom also came over and helped with laundry, Jack's room, and cleaning the living room floors. She also put plastic up around some windows to keep the heat inside this place!

Our water system also made it in yesterday. So now we have the water heater and the UV cleaning system. We are going to put that in and then worry about the rust remover system when we come back home. So I have to get the laundry room clean where we are going to be putting this system. That is NOT going to be a fun task. Apparently, I'm a pack rat. Who knew? :)

I feel as if I need to work extra hard and extra fast due to the fact that Lucy's procedure could be moved up to Friday. That is great, but if it is, I have to drive through the aftermath of this storm, and I won't be able to attend the benefit. I'm sure all our fans understand, though. I will know tomorrow if she goes in Friday or Monday. This could also mean she could very well be able to come home as early as next week! Of course it's going to depend on how her body does with the chemo and how fast it recovers afterwards. Some people take 3-4 days; others take 10. :(So, we shall see. But, this is the start of Phase 2 of our recovery no matter which way you look at it or when she gets it. Which means Phase 1 is OVER!!!

Sometimes, I have to stop and just shake my head. I can't believe how I talk about cancer like it's very matter of fact. It's crazy! But there is just so much of it all around me these days. Friends, co-workers, and yesterday, I found out one of my cousins had some cysts removed from her uterus that were cancerous. REALLY? Like one family member at a time isn't enough? They say you never get more than you can handle...well while I believe this, a little more time in between would have been nice for the family. I mean I know we are a kick ass family and all, but come on! At least let one of us win the lottery in between treating each member for cancer??? Geez! Not like we are asking for too much, right? Well, I better get off the computer and start cleaning. I seriously hate cleaning!

Day 39, Feb 2, 2011 7:35am
I was waiting until we got Lucy's numbers this morning to do a post. It seems that her ANC is down to 200, and it was 400 the other day. Dr. Pui thinks that they are still going down, which is ok... just means the chemo she had last week is still working. In order for her to get her next MRD and treatment, her ANC has to reach 500, and her WBC has to reach 1500. So she won't get her procedure Friday or Monday like we thought. It will be sometime mid-week, which is ok, it just delays us coming home a bit. And that is still an unknown number or time frame -- it's dependent upon her numbers, certain amount of days, and Pui's instinct. ;) And remember, he is never wrong.

So, I will have a few more days at home to finish up things, which is nice because we are snowed in here in Illinois, and I didn't do anything but laundry yesterday! Ha! I played video games and watched movies with Jack. I will head back down to TN on Sunday; that should be plenty of time to clear roadways.

I still hate nighttime even though I'm home. I just read a book called "The Confession" by John Grisham. In there is a man on death row, and he explains it as being worse at nighttime when all the lights are out. I know I am not in that situation, but the words he used to describe it were perfect. There isn't the hustle and bustle going on, no light, and in my case, it's quiet. Gives me time to think, which is never very good. I know she will be alright, and I know we will get through this without a doubt, but it still breaks my heart to see my little girl have to go through this. And not just

2 Kids, A Taco, And Cancer

her, but my husband who is far away and my 5 year old who cries every time he chats with his sister online because he misses her so much.

The support is great, and other families in this situation have reached out to me, and that is nice. I like to chat with them about what to expect and information on the logistics of everything, but I cannot, for some reason, read about their stories yet. Whether they are good, bad, or the same as ours. I just don't want to know because then I would compare Lucy's journey to theirs, and the one thing I have learned, every St. Jude Warrior has a different journey. And plus when I read other families' experiences, it really makes me cry. Heck, I can't even go back and read our story. I've tried. One day, I will be able to read it and hopefully return the favor of offering comfort and information to other families who go through this. And while that is sad, it is a truth. This will continue to happen to other families. I am a part of a "club" now. A club I wish I never would have had to join, but now that I am in, I have a responsibility, and plan on paying my dues after we are through our ordeal.

I also got snippy with Zach this morning via text. UGH. I just hate not being down there and asking my own questions, so he has to ask them for me, or he has already heard the answer. And then he tells me he can't give me answers because there is no one specific answer to some of my questions. Which is the no planning thing again about leukemia. I know we can't plan specifics right now around her treatment (drives me CRAZY), but it also makes it hard to plan things at home.

I have Jack here, and I think he could do ok for about 5 days without us, but any longer is a no go. He is too emotional right now, and me being home for the last two weeks has made a huge difference in his behavior from the first day I got home, and I don't want to mess that up for the poor kid. Then, I have to choose again between my two children. Lucy needs us more now than she ever has, but then again if you look at it, so does Jack. GRRRR. If she doesn't get to come home after her next high dose mex and MRD, I am going to insist that Zach trade places with me. Or I'm going to start flying down there for visits. The 16 hour drive back and forth kills me… especially all alone.

Sorry, I guess my bad night has carried over to today. Stress level today has a 100% chance of high! Along with the wind! So I'll stay indoors, keep warm, and take my regular dose of Xanax in a timely manner.

Day 41, Feb 4, 2011 6:17am
Man, I was so busy yesterday that I was too tired at the day's end to write a journal entry. It is nice to be busy; helps keep your mind on the goal. The end product. The cure. I feel for my husband who does not have this luxury of being "separated" from Lucy for a moment to think. When she goes to bed at 9, he is in the same room with the lights out, and not much to do. I know he has played his DS, and has watched some Netflix, but believe it or not, when you have the opportunity to watch all the movies you want and play video games all night, it's not as fun. I can't wait for him and Lu to be home so we can tuck our children into bed and relax in the living room after they are out.

I remember the first time Jack slept in his own bed as a baby. Prior to that, he slept in our room next to our bed. Zach decided he needed to use his crib because it had been long enough. So we put him into his bed; he didn't fuss or complain, and we gently closed the door and stared at one another and sighed. While he was just in the other room, it was as if this huge brick had been lifted from our shoulders. The barrier of the door to his room was all we needed to exhale and have some "me" time. I said "What do we do now?" And I remember exactly what we did. We made root beer floats and watched a movie. It was awesome. We said "So this is what our parents did after we went to bed; enjoyed themselves". Knowing how important this down time is, I feel for my husband who doesn't have that right now. Neither of us did while we were at the RMH.

Today, Jack goes back to school! Yea!! I say that, and I haven't checked the school closings yet. HA! They better have school; there is no reason not to. I love my child, but yesterday he was even telling me I was getting on his last nerve. :) Stinker.

I got the laundry room clean and all ready for my Uncle Andy to come over and install our water system this morning. THAT was a task. UGH! Funny how when you are cleaning and organizing things that you don't normally do, the rest of your house become a mess. The center is now what I need to concentrate on. I bought a Shark steamer and used it last night for about an hour and got our cabinets clean along with our counters, etc., and I'll be darned if it doesn't work wonderfully. I'll finish "the center" today and steam clean some more stuff. I also ran errands yesterday because we were out of things like garbage bags, dish soap, and some food staples, and I worked from home. My arms were sore because I had shoveled the steps in front of our house for 20 minutes. Yep, that's all I did. Then my wonderful neighbors came by with a snow blower and a 12-pack and finished it up! By 11:30pm I was mentally and physically exhausted, so I slept hard.

Since I have been home, I have had to do a lot of things that I would normally let Zach do. So he said to me last night, "You are totally giving yourself away". I told him, "Hey, I was independent for 29 years before meeting you and did everything for myself. After you came along, it was a perk to have the help ;)". I am seriously proud of some of my skills! Ha! Although, I will welcome him home and pretend not to know how to do things soon.

My children talked on the phone last night, and I do believe I have the sweetest babies on earth. Lucy said, "Jack, you missing me?" Jack said, "Of course, I am!" Then Lucy said, "I love you, Jack". They miss each other so much!! I never realized how much they played until they aren't together. Jack is in constant need of redirection and things to do, whereas before, they entertained one another; whether it was playing or fighting, they were a team! Jack told her, "Lucy, I think you only have one cancer bug left". She was thrilled! She said, "REALLY, JACK!!!! Just ONE more".

Lucy goes in today to get her blood work that will determine exactly when she gets her next MRD and high dose methotrexate.

That will also determine when I return to Memphis. I'm thinking I will leave Monday morning, but I will know more later today. If her procedure is Tuesday, then I'm definitely leaving Monday; if it's not until Wednesday or Thursday, then I may hold off a day, so I can be with Jack an extra day. I'm not sure how long I will be gone, so I am trying to minimize the time being away from Jack as best as possible.

Tomorrow is our benefit in Lexington. I explained to Jack what a benefit was all about; not sure he grasped the concept fully. We will be there tomorrow early and stay as long as he is entertained. :) I hope to see everybody there and thank them personally for all the support and donations. We truly feel very lucky and appreciate the effort everybody has put into this. It is an all ages event; doors open at 6 at the Lexington Community Center, tickets can be purchased at the door, and entertainment starts at 7. And there is some really AWESOME entertainment!!! We feel lucky to have musician friends because music soothes the soul.

Day 41, Feb 4, 2011 8:36pm
Greetings from Memphis. Zach here...

Today, we did our blood tests again. They were good and bad. The one thing I learned today is to not look for the light at the end of the tunnel. Right now, my "light" has been to go home. The whole time here in Memphis, I've been so far from going home, that I never thought about it. But now we are "closer". This is good, because it means we will soon be moving into our next phase of treatment. But it's bad because it sets expectations and raises hope of leaving. This causes me to lose sight of the real goal. All day yesterday, I was waiting for blood tests and working with Shawna on logistics for Lucy's next procedure. Today was a reminder that you can't plan more than 48 hours in advance. I've been reminded not to plan for next Wednesday, but to be planning for tonight, tomorrow, and possibly Sunday.

Most of Lucy's numbers have bottomed out and started to climb again. This is good. Her ANC is up to 300; her WBC is climbing. Hemoglobin is also up. But for some reason, her platelets sunk like a pirate's treasure. So low in fact, that she needs another transfusion. BUT, we didn't do it.

Dr. Pui explained that if we give her a transfusion, it's going to skew her numbers a good deal. We would need a week to recover from the transfusion to see where her numbers really are. Apparently, giving her someone else's blood platelets can mask her blood counts. On Wednesday, her platelets were 44,000 and today they were 19,000. They do transfusions below 20,000. A count of 100,000 is required for her next procedure and the start of our next phase of treatment. WBC needs to be 1500, ANC needs to be at least 300, and the Dr. Pui factor also needs to be high.

Originally, our procedure was going to be this coming Monday. Then, they said Tuesday or Wednesday. Now, they are saying Wednesday or later. So as you can see, there's no real way to plan for this. No way to see 48 hours ahead of yourself. And when you remind yourself of that, then it's really not all that bad. You know what you need to do, you're not looking forward to a "leave date" only to watch it pass, and you concentrate on spending the current day with your daughter.

Sunday night, we are going to go in at 6:30pm to get blood taken. If her platelets are lower, they'll do a transfusion and give us a week for her numbers to stabilize. We will talk to Dr. Pui Monday morning.

The issue with the platelet's, of course, is bleeding. Her little red spots are returning as a result. They are like little freckles all over her body. This is normal, but we are at a high risk for bleeding. I am to check her urine, examine her butt, and look for blood leaking from her eyes. Quite a to-do list compared to my last one (get Christmas gifts, take out the trash, and add salt to the softener).

They did relax her diet today! No low bacteria diet for a few days is kind of nice. I ordered a pizza right away. She'll be back on the low bacteria diet when her methotrexate starts.

Today in the hospital, someone handed me an envelope. In it was $30. No note, no reason. The messenger slipped up, and I found out who it was. It was one of the nurses. I don't know why she did it, but I wasn't supposed to know. Why $30? Why anything? And why us? I'm not sure on any of that. It really confused me, but at the same time showed how much people care for Lucy. It was extremely generous, and I used it to buy the pizza tonight! Ha-ha. Lucy was so excited to eat bread sticks and have "dip". I'll get that nurse back though. I'm not sure how, but I'll figure out something creative. The funny thing is that it wasn't even one of the "front line" nurses that's in our room every day. But, she is a nurse that Lucy runs to every day and gives a big hug.

I had a 30 minute meeting with Dr. Pui to talk about our next phase of treatment. I learned quite a bit and will talk more about it once I read through it all. It's a book. But here's some things that stuck in my mind:
1) Only 11 spinal taps left to be done (All in Memphis)
2) Be in Memphis no less that once every 8 weeks
3) Reinduction 2 might be done in Peoria
4) 30% chance of lifelong damage to short term memory
5) 2% chance of stroke
6) 7% change of pancreatitis (I have no idea how to spell that, sorry).
7) No calendar or schedule is given for the reasons mentioned above.
8) IF her MRD is 0.000, she's considered low risk, and falls into the 99% survival group, but they won't stamp her as low risk until the MRD is gone. Lucy still says she has 2 cancers bugs left, but I think she's wrong. I think they are all gone now.

Once we do her next MRD, she gets high dose Methotrexate. That will happen here in Memphis 4 times, every 14 days, and we will leave each time when it clears her system. So if it takes 5 days to clear the first time, we will get 7 days home (because we need to check into the hospital on the 13th day).

After that, well, who cares. That's way too far ahead of time.

Right now, I'm concentrating on tomorrow. And some friends of ours get to leave tomorrow. Alanis is a little girl that Lucy met down her. She's a sweet little girl who is 6 years old. She has a different diagnosis than us and is able to go back to California to continue her treatment there. It's exciting to see people that get to go home on good terms.

Tonight, while Lucy was doing her IV meds, we went down and made a Valentine's Day mailbox. It was fun, and she was excited to leave the room. We've also been doing art projects every day in the waiting room at the hospital. She LOVES glue. And requires a LOT of it. The projects at the hospital are usually locked up until 8 or 8:30, so I've made sure to pack markers, crayons, and paper for our early appointments. The best part about doing projects there is that once your name is called, you leave. It's not like at home where you sweep up sparkles and pick Play Doh out of the floors for 3 days. :)

Tomorrow, I plan on scavenging through Alanis' family's stuff they leave behind. When people leave, they usually leave some stuff in the pantry. Top items: spoons, bowls, and bottled water. One family gave us frozen pizzas when they left. It was awesome. I guess it's the little things that rock.

On the home front, some of the water system was installed today. There was a problem with the glass for the UV light, so there's a bit of delay there. but at least all the plumbing is in place. That will at least make the water safe enough to take a bath in. There are still some more components that will need to be addressed in the near future. New media in the softener, solution for the high iron content, and a solution for high tannins. All are important and can have detrimental effects on the UV system, but won't need to be fixed before she returns home. But, will need to be corrected quickly.

Personally, I feel better today than yesterday. Sometimes it gets pretty lonely when the lights go out at 8:30, and you are left with nothing but your thoughts and about 4 hours before you can fall asleep. But today for some reason, I don't feel the late night blues.

Must mean I'm taking enough medication. Hahahah.

Today's post is pretty much all over the board, and not formatted in any way. Excuse the spelling (Not using spell check). And for some reason, there seems to be a lack of humor. I'm usually a little more smart-ass-ish. So I apologize for lack of comic material. Oh, and I failed English class in High School so many times, that at one point I was taking 3 classes of English in the same semester. So my writing probably needs a little work. (That's a true story). Carry On. Zach

Day 43, Feb 6, 2011 7:36am
As I type, I do believe my feet are swollen to a size bigger than normal. Last night was the benefit for Lucy, and I don't think I sat down for the first 5 hours. AMAZING!!! AMAZING!!! AMAZING! That is all I can say. I now know what people mean when they say words cannot express how thankful I am. And ''ts true. How do you say thank you when people have given you the biggest gift and in your most time of need. So all I can think of is this: Thank you.

I got there a little after 6, and couldn't believe the line going out the door. It started at 6, but the room was already packed and filling up. The bands, Chris Corkery, Under the Gun, and Hillbilly Jones, were awesome! The volunteers who put this thing together were incredible. I saw them running around and making sure everything ran smoothly, and at one point, I heard somebody say (and I won't mention names, Deanna) "I don't work this hard at my job." :) And I'm proud that we ran out of beer and somebody had to run not once, but TWICE, to get more. Good job! But yet, there was still food available. :)

The basket auctions were incredibly put together, and people really were generous with the services and products they donated. The 50/50 was humbling. People kept buying tickets and then giving them to me. My dad ended up winning, and giving me the money. Thanks, Dad. I will make sure I don't hit you up for money for a long time. ;) And my brother, Kevin, and sister in law, Molly, were kind enough to take Jack home with them so I could make sure I personally thanked as many people as possible. If I missed you, I'm sorry, and thank you ((hugs)).

I wore boots with a slight heel...big mistake! Lesson learned. I saw so many great people that I haven't seen in years, and I can't tell you how many strangers I met for the first time who came because they were so touched by my Lucy. I can't count how many hugs I received; that was awesome. And at one point, the community center was standing room only in both of the rooms and out the hallway. Truly more than we could have ever asked for or expected. Thank you!

I did ask to use the microphone so I could thank everybody for their support (I secretly wanted to just use the microphone and sing), and anybody that knows me knows I am never at a loss for words, but just in case I froze, I wrote down what I wanted to say and read it out loud. I practiced it 5 times the night before so I could get through it without crying, and by the 5th time I was good, but when I got up in front of all those people, I cried anyhow. I would like to share what I wrote with all of our supporters.

What Cancer has taught me.

1. There is nothing a parent would not do for their child
2. The strong willed attitude that my Lucy possesses was all for a reason from the start, and that will get her through this
3. Planning is not an option with Cancer
4. I miss sleeping in the same bed with my husband
5. Support from friends, family, and even strangers is humbling and amazing
6. Lucy CAN and WILL eat 5 hotdogs in one sitting when given steroids
7. Jack is a strong young boy, who has a kind heart and unconditional love for his sister
8. Even when they say "this hospital has good food", they are lying
9. Hand sanitizer is actually good for you to use and can be addictive

10. Lucy never complains about waiting. Waiting to see doctors, waiting to get chemo, waiting to go home.

11. LUCY is amazing

12. It has reaffirmed what I already suspected: I married the most caring, gentle, and kind man

13. Ramen noodles aren't just for broke college kids; they are for broke families enduring cancer treatments as well

14. Eat when you get a chance; there may not be another chance in a while

15. Same for sleep. Sleep when you can; you may miss your opportunity

16. A 3 year old girl CAN poop at least 8 times a day

17. We will no longer complain about our 1200 sq foot home; it's a mansion

18. It is really hard to yell at a bald cancer patient

19. The Beatles ARE rock stars

20. Lucy is Amazing

21. Shaving off all of your little girl's hair is very emotional, even when you think you are prepared

22. Technology is a wonderful tool to have when your family is 500 miles apart

23. Our family has a wonderfully sick sense of humor

24. I hate cleaning

25. Dr. Pui is an angel and deserves a Nobel peace prize for his efforts and strides he has accomplished with defeating childhood cancer

26. Danny Thomas should be spoken of right up there with Ghandi and Martin Luther King

27. St. Jude is heaven on earth

28. Sleeping in a 12x12 room with your two children for a week is possible without hurting somebody

29. Despite the fighting and yelling and practically killing one another, my children are BFFs

30. The Ronald McDonald House was the best idea ever invented for parents with sick children.

31. There is nothing more important than family and everything else is just a bonus

32. No matter how bad you think your life is,

somebody is always going through something worse, even cancer. And....last....

33. My Lucy is absolutely amazing

Day 44, Feb 7, 2011 5:21am

Zach took Lucy in last night to get labs done before she sees Pui this morning, and we are stoked because her platelets are rising as well as all the rest of her numbers! Yea! That will mean no transfusion!! At least we hope; sometimes Pui throws a wild card at you. But no transfusions means as soon as her platelets hit 100,000, she can get her next MRD (tells us if the cancer is in remission) along with starting the next phase of chemo, which only gets us that much closer to recovery and coming home!

So after she sees Pui this morning, we will have more of an idea when she will be going in. The other part of not being able to plan is what we call "the Pui Factor". Everybody always tells us where her numbers need to be for certain things, or a timeframe of how things are done, but then they say "You have to wait and see what Pui does though". Apparently, he has good instincts. So she sees him at 9 this morning, and I will know more then, but I am planning on packing my bags and heading down to Memphis tomorrow morning bright and early.

I told Jack I was leaving, and he said, "Ok, that's fine, but how long will you be gone?" I told him I wasn't sure. I said I could be gone for 5 days or 10, and he said he was ok with it this time. I think he's probably second guessing me coming home and disciplining him! Hahahah! He's probably going back in his mind and thinking "Why did I ever wish her back when the gma's let me do anything I want?"

So yesterday was almost more overwhelming for me emotionally than Saturday was. I was recapping the night; we got preliminary totals, and I was just humbled and amazed at the support. Then we got pictures back from several different cameras, and it was cool to see how packed it was and pictures of everybody having a great time. The other thing I noticed is that the pictures (from different cameras) were filled with orbs (bubbles of light). And some folks may say it was the dust particles or lighting, but I am one of those who truly believes that we were all surrounded by an aura that is bigger than ourselves. Some people say ghosts, some say angels, and I truly believe it was "something". Not sure what. And to see them in a ton of the pictures was pretty emotional for me, and I can't explain why because I'm not sure why. It's the spiritual aspect I think. Pretty cool, all in all.

Today will be a day of packing, getting my refrigerator in, and last minute errand running for the house since I'm not sure how long I'll be gone.

I'm anxious to see Lucy and Zach. I video chatted with them last night and Lucy is definitely going back to looking like herself (minus the hair of course). :) Her cheeks are going down a bit. She looks SOOO good. I'm anxious for her next chemo and procedure because that will tell us if the cancer is in total remission. The chemo may make her super sick; they say even with the Zofran, this one tends to make them throw up a lot. I hate seeing her throw up and being miserable. So, I want to get this poison in and out of her little body quick! And along the way, they can take every nasty cell that looks like it might change to cancer with them!!!
I also think I'm anxious for leaving Jack and not having a timeframe for when I'm coming back. Man, today might be an extra Xanax day. I don't think I anticipated all of the anxious feelings I would have about what the next phase of treatment means. I will keep everybody posted on when we hear the news.

Day 44, Feb 7, 2011 12:17pm
Ok, Lucy has seen Pui this morning, and she goes in for her next procedure and high dose Methotrexate on Wednesday morning. We go into clinic the night before to get IV fluids. The average inpatient time is anywhere from 2-4 days. They told us it was about 50/50 on when we get to come home-home. Sometimes its 2-4 days, others its 6-7 days after treatment. Best case scenario, we drive her home Sunday; worst case next Tuesday. Then, she will be home for 6 days and then we will fly back to Memphis to do

this all over again. I'm thankful we *may* get to come home at all!! Even if just for a visit. I plan on heading out bright and early tomorrow!

Day 45, Feb 8, 2011 7:02am
So I'm up and drinking coffee...need to make sure I drink enough to make the 7 hour trek. I could hardly sleep last night because I'm so excited to see my Lucy and Zach. Plus, I started have a running nose yesterday and am worried it's a cold. :(This morning, it seems to be a little stuffy, but it's just one side of my face, so it could very well just be sinus draining or allergies (I have the worst time with allergies in the WINTER!! who does that??). Anyhow, Zach said, "Just wash your hands, and we will be fine".

I wanted to post an update only because last night was a good night for our family. First, I had a teacher from Little Jewels (Jack's daycare before kindergarten) drop off some money and a gift basket. They held silent auctions at the school, and the staff and parents bid on items to help us raise money. Truly AMAZING!! And then the parent who won the "Date Night" basket paid for it and said she didn't want it because we had way more stress in our lives than she would ever. I got goose bumps, and later as I went through the basket, it made me tear up. People have been fantastic to us through this whole thing. I am looking forward to the day when it is all over and we can return the favor and pay it forward.

The other awesome thing is Lucy got a makeover last night by Miss Tennessee and the runner up, Miss Erin (I think was her name). She was tickled pink. She got a boa, a tiara, they painted her nails, AND she got make up!! She got blush, eye shadow, and lip-gloss, all of which she got to keep. Zach said at first she was shy, but then she warmed up to them. I posted the new pic as our wall picture here, and if you want to see the video, Zach uploaded it to YouTube. Just subscribe to his channel: weberzach.

I talked to her on the phone and she was thrilled and told me she was a "real princess". Then I got to video chat with her later, and she just didn't want to hang up. Longest chat yet!!! And she looks

AWESOME! Her Lucy face is definitely coming back along with her voice. She's also learning words to 2 new Beatles songs "Ticket to Ride" and "You're Gonna Lose That Girl". So sweet. She sang for me.

Zach texted me later and said "Apparently, Lucy was on the local news here getting her make over". We have been searching online to find a clip and can't. I may have to just email the news station to get that. Our little celebrity. :)

Well, I better get ready to head off to Memphis. It's funny cuz they are under a winter storm warning, and it's not supposed to hit until tomorrow and it's like 2-3 inches of snow! BWAHAHAHA! I was watching the news down there last night (trying to find Lucy's story), and the weather man was showing pictures of downtown Memphis and saying "See, there is still snow on the ground". It was a light dusting. :) And they were saying the frigid temps of 32 degrees were killing them. Which I know when you aren't used to it, I bet it is. But I had to chuckle and say "try -10, dude".
Until next time.....

Day 46, Feb 9, 2011 9:27am
Waiting to go in for MRD, spinal, and high dose Methotrexate. Will be admitted immediately following. Will post more once some results are back.

Rub some dirt on it / You'll be fine.

Day 47, Feb 10, 2011 7:38am
Yesterday was a long and, for some odd reason, a very emotional day for me. I was anxious. Anxious about every little thing. Lucy had her appointment with Pui, then we had to wait for procedure, spinal tap, MRD, and Methotrexate. Which wasn't a biggie. They had valentines for her to do while she waited.

And you want to talk about a girl using glitter!! Oh my! Glitter and glue!

Then we went in, and I could see the stress on Zach's face. He hates when they put her under. They were asking us if the stuff they used last time worked well, and we said she was agitated when she woke up, but we weren't sure if that was from the PPrednisone she was on or not. So while she had her procedure, Zach and I ate lunch. Then, when she woke up, we were there.

She didn't sleep as long after this procedure, so when we went in, she was still very wobbly and would just fall asleep. Then, the agitation and anger started. That was our first clue the Prednisone was not what caused this. It was the drugs. Then, we wheeled her down in the red wagon to A clinic to let our nurse, Justine, know we were ready to be admitted. They didn't have any beds open, so we were going to be put in ICU only because it was an open bed. While we were waiting, she was throwing up. So we definitely know next time to try a different drug before procedure.

As we were getting ready to go to our bed, we got the call that a room had opened up on the 4th floor, which is the leukemia floor. Thank goodness! We weren't keen to be in ICU and all that entailed. It took another 3 hours for us to get upstairs, and we found out the only bed open was isolation. Which isn't a huge deal, but nervous being in a confined area, where across the hall, a child is in isolation for a reason and has a communicable disease if some sort. They have doors that separate us, but still close!!

So we were ready for her to start her high dose Methotrexate which runs for 24 hours, but the ph was off in her urine so we had to get meds to level that out and wait. I was very impatient and frustrated by this time, and I'm not sure why. I've waited longer for things. I think the idea of home is so close, that I need to just put that out of my mind and focus on the here and now; you would think I would have learned, but no. Still planning! Argh! By 9 pm, her drip was finally started.

So here is how this works: she gets the Methotrexate for 24 hours. They will do blood checks on the 23rd hour and 42nd hour to see if her system is clearing the drug. Methotrexate at these doses is bad on the kidneys, thus the inpatient for the first round for two days, and we are to encourage her to drink and pee as much as possible. If at the 42nd hour, they are comfortable with her levels and her other numbers haven't crashed, they will release us to go home-home. That is why I think I'm so damn anxious. Home is so close. And Zach says I need to not get my hopes up, and I know he's right, but dammit, for once I want to look forward to something good! Argh.

We got her roadmap for this next phase of treatment. I should be thrilled to death because we are all done with Phase 1!! Yea!! Phase 2 is called Consolidation. She gets these spinals and high dose Methotrexate every two weeks, and if in between her numbers are good, we get the 7-10 day home visit. I should also be thrilled because for the first time ever, Dr. Pui said Lucy was low risk! We had heard she may be, but he never said it out loud until yesterday. He said if her MRD comes back negative, she stays in low risk; if it comes back positive, we will be looking at an entirely different protocol. We will know in 1-3 days.

I am not sure why I had such a rough night and why I was fighting with my husband over text. I think it's because I've been home, and while that doesn't change the fact my Lu has cancer, I was busy all the time. Being here and waiting and seeing why you're here and being reminded that all these children are sick, quite simply sucks.

Whew! That was a lot!! But now that I've got it all out and cried it out last night, I'm good to go. Put yesterday behind me and move forward to today, and today only.

CHAPTER 5
REMISSION AND HOME

Day 48, Feb 11, 2011 7:01am

Last night, Lucy finished her high dose Methotrexate at 9:20! Woo hoo!!! Only three more of those to go in Phase 2. Too bad each and every dose can give her different reactions at different times. But I'm thankful that so far the first one has given her no problems. She was up last night in her baggy underwear singing Beyonce. We will find out her level this morning and see how well her kidneys are flushing it through. And today is the day to find out if and when we can go HOME for a little break!! Woo hoo!! See... all my planning has worked out! Ha-ha that was a joke! Even just being able to go home to RMH and not be inpatient will be nice because she is bored to tears!!

Short update today, but check back later as I will post updates as we receive them!! Think good thoughts!!

Day 48, Feb 11, 2011 5:08pm

She is cancer free!!!!!!!!!!! Dr Pui said she is in the almost 100% cure rate!!!!!!! Woo hoo!!!!! Home-home tomorrow!!!!!!!!

Day 49, Feb 12, 2011 7:17am

What an unbelievable and emotional day yesterday; for the good this time! I'm still blown away and thrilled her MRD came back negative.

It was kind of funny how we found out, too. We were getting ready to be discharged and were on our way home-home anyhow. They had said the results from the MRD weren't in, but they would call us Monday at home. So we were thrilled they were going to let us go home. Then, as the pharmacist was going over her meds, the nurse popped her head in and said MRD is negative. 0.0 cancer cells.

I wanted to scream and cry and dance and felt like I should be shouting it off the rooftop! So, after the pharmacist left, we went into Lucy's room and I was dancing and singing and telling her she worked so hard that she got every last one of those stinking cancer bugs!!! She said in a question tone, "I have zero?" I said, "Yes baby!!! All gone!" She said, "I can go home-home???" And it was the best feeling ever to tell her yes!!!!

Zach and I were going to go downstairs to make sure we told our family and saw Pui in the hallway. He said "Emily stole my thunder!" Hahha!! So, we followed him to the room. He looked at Lucy, and I saw a smile on that man's face the entire time he was in there, which is a first.

He asked Lucy if he could have a kiss and said another lady had kissed him that day too -- Marlo Thomas. So he said two great ladies had given him kisses: Lucy and Marlo. What great company he had that day! And what a privilege and honor for us to have him as a doctor. He looked at us casually and said "She is in almost 100% cure rate." Woo hoo!!!!!! Cure!!!!!

Lucy knows that we aren't done with treatment. We asked her what she needs to do next, and she replied, "Teach my body to make plain blood." She asked, "Where did the cancer bugs go? In the garbage??" And I said, "They are probably in the sewer, and dead." Then, my sweet caring little girl said "Well, they need to make it back home to their families.". Here she is concerned about the damn cancer! Did you know that my Lucy is destined for great things?

Yesterday was also awesome because I did a live interview on the radio to tell Lucy's story to help raise money for the Ronald McDonald House. This is one of the only houses where it is completely FREE to families. And they live on donations only. I was super nervous and got choked up a bit. My good friend Patty had written an e-mail to the DJs who read it out loud on the air while I was on. Thank God!! She said exactly what I needed to hear to help relax me a bit. After we got back to the RMH, the manager told me that within 20 min of my interview, $10,000 came in for donations. I was floored. Not sure if it was anything I said or just timing, but I will always believe it was Lucy's story that touched people's hearts.

We came back to the RMH, and Lucy got her loving from Debbie, the house manager. And she didn't let her put her down!! Suckered her into playing for over an hour! And it was her evening off. That is the one thing I wanted to mention in my interview... the staff. Because while the free rooms and free food and proximity to the hospital are great, the staff is the best feature.

So, we are going home today! We started packing last night and ran out of bags and energy. We gave all our leftover food to a family, because lord knows, we aren't taking it with us and it's easier for us to get groceries at home than it is for somebody here. Plus, this family gave us all their food when they went home the first time. Paying them back. We also weeded through some of Lucy's things that she either had double of or weren't open that we got from the hospital and put it in the "free" box for another child who wasn't as fortunate as us to have so much support. So off I go to finish packing!!!!

Day 50, Feb 13, 2011 5:46am
Home home home home home home home home home home!!! It was awesome to wake up in my own bed with my husband and Taco. Of course, Zach was a cover stealer all night! LOL! And Taco kept laying on my legs... but I wouldn't have it any other way.

It's so funny how Lucy just fell right back into routine and her old little self again. She was playing with every one of her toys, and she and Jack were running from room to room and chasing each other and playing games and coloring. It's like they have a TON to make up for....and they do. It was sweet music to my ears to listen to them giggle and scream and play together all night long. Then at relaxing time, she yelled at Jack about sharing! Hahahah! So that is normal and GREAT!! And she could not be happier when we tucked her into bed. She stayed in her room and sang to her babies until she fell asleep. It was so sweet to hear that noise coming from her room.

It's a little nerve racking to think that we have to keep her in this bubble, and our house is much bigger than our room at the RMH, so we have to keep it clean too. And we realized last night how much harder that will be with two kids, toys, and of course, the dirt tracked inside the house. My mom had scrubbed the floors before we came home; I had done it before we left, and when I saw the bottom of my son's feet yesterday I was like "Yikes! GERMS!!!" They were black and nasty!! It was because we were coming in and out and carrying stuff in from the truck. So, definitely going to be a new stress for us. When we left, Lucy's ANC had dropped to 800 on Friday from the previous 1300 on Thursday, and I'm sure its bottomed out, or pretty close by now, so now we go back on low bacteria diet and of course everything sterile. And Jack has this cough that sounds horrible. Don't think that didn't make my stomach twist and turn. But what do you do ? You have to live as a family and learn how to take what comes at you in terms of illness and bacteria. I think after we get more accustomed to it, it'll be ok; right now, we are still in shock.

So today, we make to-do lists, get ready for the week, and hopefully Zach will return to work remotely. And we get to hang out and fight with each other like a normal family! Hip-hip hooray!!

Tuesday, we go to Peoria to start our visits with the St. Jude Affiliate and learn the ropes there. Then, we return to Memphis next Tuesday to start her #2 high dose Methotrexate. We are going to enjoy our 9 days and "learn to live in our new normal."

Day 51, Feb 14, 2011 6:55am
Yesterday was a great day for Lucy. She played and fought with Jack all day. :) I had gotten up early, like usual, and it was music to my ears when I heard her yell from her room, "Mommy, I'm ready to wake up." That is something she always does, so it was nice to hear something familiar.

Her appetite is slowing returning. After having fluids for nearly 4 days, her stomach was full, so she wasn't hungry, but yesterday, she started to eat, so that was good. Not a lot, but anything is good. And she still gets chemotherapy at night, 6MP, so it can make her nauseous too. I give her Zofran right when she wakes up, but she almost yacked this morning, so I think we may want to start giving her a dose 2 hours before the meds, and then again in the morning, just to be safe.

Last night, Jack had to do valentines for school, and Lucy said, "Hey, I need to do some for my friends too." Good thing I had just bought her some last year when they went on clearance and had them on hand. She named off all the friends in daycare and made a card for each of them. She made 2 for Lisa, her daycare provider.

She keeps asking when she gets to go back to Lisa's. And we keep telling her she can't go back, but I don't think she grasps it. She misses her friends and a baby doll there she calls "big baby." Don't you love her names for her babies? As soon as we get the "ok" and her ANC reaches a good number (which could be a few months), we are definitely throwing a party with all her daycare friends so she can see them.

Last night, Zach and I cooked steaks we had in the freezer that were slated for New Years. We even got the grill out and made cheeseburgers for the kids. It was awesome. Then after the kids went to bed, we opened a bottle of Moscato and had chocolate covered strawberries to celebrate "Christmas, New Years, Zach's Birthday, Remission, AND Valentine's day" WHEW! We had a lot to celebrate.

Today, we will finish unpacking the car and are going to have to weed through Lucy's toys and clothes. Boy, she came home with more than her room can hold!! Thank you to so many people that were generous in sending her packages and toys and clothes. I'll work today, and then we have a few tweaks to make to our water system and get a few things for the air filter system.

Our water system filters the water so well, and we have so much crap in our water, that a filter that was supposed to last a month, lasted 2 days. And you should see it. It was white when it was put in, now it's so black and clogged. It's disgusting. It made our water pressure go down to nothing. So we have to find a solution to add another filter that doesn't decrease the water pressure. And we are going to get a small HEPA system that will help with dust. Our furnace works great, but it filters when its running, and it doesn't run all the time, so we need something to help with dust. We have all wood floors, and if you have them, you know how much dust can gather in one day and float in the air because it has nowhere to "land". So that is what Zach is going to do today.

Tomorrow we go to Peoria for our first visit there. we are anxious to see her numbers, it's odd not being able to see them every other day!!

Day 51, Feb 14, 2011 8:03pm
Greetings from Bloomington. Zach here. Being home is quite a bit different from Memphis. It feels quite weird. In Memphis, every night when you leave the hospital, you get a schedule. The schedule tells you everything you are doing the following day. It determined nap, breakfast, lunch, and dinner. By looking at your schedule, you had an idea of what type of activities to bring, both for yourself and Lucy. You had a schedule that told when the shuttle left each location. You had daily printouts of blood statistics (which I would trend daily). It was kind of like a medical boot camp.

Sunday, I stood around with a blank stare. It was the first day in about 50 days that I had any control over anything, and it was weird. No schedule. No direction. It definitely took a minute to get used to.

We still have some household issues to take care of though. Like Shawna mentioned before, our water system clogged up. Ninety dollars later, and I have some different filters arriving on Wednesday. I think it will take a little trial and error, and maybe some more equipment, before we get all the kinks worked out. But I will say: for the 2 days we had water, it sure was clear. Usually, it's an orange color. Kind of like juice.

When Lucy went down for nap time, she started yelling about a bloody nose. And sure enough, I ran in, and she REALLY had a bloody nose. Since her platelets aren't like yours and mine, her nose bleeds can look like a murder scene. And they take a while to stop. And last night, around 1:00AM I woke up to hear Lucy having one of her nightmares.

The chemo really seems to give her night terrors. It also makes her pretty sick; I'm worried she'll get sick at night, and nobody will hear it. So I went to Toys R Us today and bought a baby monitor. What a strange feeling. Even though we have passed the baby stage, we are definitely in a parallel universe. Instead of listening for crying for a bottle, we're listening for vomiting.

Oh, and baby monitors have changed since the last time I bought one. This thing is digital and even has a button on the "parent side" that allows me to yell at Lucy without even getting out of bed. Now that's a great use of technology. Before, when she was screwing around at bedtime, I had to go open her door and scare her. Now I can just hit the button. :)

Tomorrow, we go to Peoria for her first blood tests since Friday. I'm assuming her ANC has crashed, and they'll tweak her 6MP chemo. If that's the case, she'll be back on a low bacteria diet. Dr. Pui said we would be good eating like "regular people" until her next blood tests. His only rule was to use good judgment and not to let her eat off the floor. Little does he know, Lucy will eat food from ANYWHERE. Especially off the floor! She'll eat anything. So here we are... Working especially hard to jack-up everything Dr. Pui and St. Jude has done.

Right now; I'm exhausted. It's a ton of work being home, and there's still a lot to be done. The car needs brakes. I need a root canal. I need to get back to work. The water system needs tweaked. We head back to Memphis on Monday. Brakes will get done, but root canal will have to wait.

Anyway, tomorrow will be nice to get our intro to the Peoria St. Jude. I'm hoping for no blood transfusions and high ANC, platelets, and WBC. Rub some dirt on it / you'll be fine

Day 52, Feb 15, 2011 7:40am

So, today is our first Peoria visit as Zach referenced, and I'm so nervous. I have butterflies. For 3 days we were "normal," and now back to the grind. It's comforting and nerve wracking all at once. Being home is definitely a different normal. Like the baby monitor, and me constantly having to see where she is at all times because I'm just nervous like that. Then there is the nosebleed that Zach mentioned. UGH... that scared the crap out me and I was ready to take her to Peoria. It's like bringing home your FIRST newborn baby. You are scared to death, don't know what to do, glad to be home, but just want to hurry up and "learn" everything and get comfortable.

Then there is the clean house...that is a total joke! 2 kids and a dog... try chasing them around and keeping it clean... not easy. All while working and still unpacking a truck full of stuff. Then finding space for everything? We definitely need some storage options here! Ha! And I'm not talking about pick up clean, I mean scrubbed, Clorox-clean. It's not working out very smoothly. I keep the kitchen clean and Cloroxed, as well as the bathroom, but anything else just keeps getting put on the back burner. I can't believe this place was spotless a week ago.

I'm home waiting for the bus to pick Jack up; then I will head to Peoria. Daddy and Lucy already left. We have to drive separately because we have to make sure somebody is here to see Jack off and to see him home just in case she needs blood today; that could take HOURS. I'm hoping it's a quick trip, her numbers are on the rise, and we can exhale....

Day 53, Feb 16, 2011 4:59am

Wow, I'm up before my alarm went off. Of course, I crashed at 9 last night. Sounds like normal to me! I haven't gone to bed that early since before the leukemia. And last night was about as normal as its been in a long time, even with our trip to Peoria and getting a blood transfusion!

The kids played and chased each other around the house; Jack was an awesome big brother and was helping Lucy to make a journal like the one he has at school. We ate dinner around the table and yelled at the kids about good manners. Then, we all did our own thing afterwards until bed time. The kids watched Superman, I worked on thank you notes (which I think I'll be doing for the next 3 years just to get caught up), and Zach cleaned up the dinner mess and started laundry.

I'm still a nervous wreck when the kids play and roughhouse a bit. I have to stop that quick. I know Lucy's platelets are good, but it's still not a good idea to have her get hurt right now. And I still need for her to be where I can see her almost 100% of the time or I freak out, but all in all... normal.

We did go to our first clinic in Peoria. All we heard from folks down in Memphis and other families is that Peoria is an awesome affiliate, and that we were so lucky to be close to that. So my impression of Peoria: spot on to their comments, but still it's not familiar, so it's a bit strange. The facility is awesome. We walk into the waiting room where children are all set up with their IVs, chemo, fluids, blood, etc. and playing games, Wii, using play-doh, and normal kid things. There is a counter set up with food to eat while you wait, and the parents fill the chairs that outline the room. I finally got to meet one parent who had contacted me when this first started. Her son, Nicholas, also has leukemia, and they are from Hudson. Odd, never have met her in person, but you wouldn't know it by the conversations we had. And the nurses were super nice and very knowledgeable. They are bit more relaxed than in Memphis and will even admit that to you.

Our doctor said that Pui is super-strict and during induction that is good, and that we still need to be careful, but can be a little more lax at home. That was a comfort. We were really concerned about the whole "get her to the hospital in 45 minutes with a fever" thing. We are at least an hour door to door, so that worried us, but she said an hour was fine. Just get in the car and call us on the way over if we run into that situation. Hopefully we won't, but have to be prepared. And kids get fevers, chemo, cancer... no chemo, no cancer. We have to remember this.

Lucy has also had a nose bleed every day since Memphis and even two times a day, so we had the doc take a look. It comes from what we suspected. Dry air and picking it! She keeps telling me, "But mom, I have to get the crumbs out". I told her its dry blood and that the "crumbs" will always be there if she doesn't stop picking them. I told her she needs to let them come out on their own. She doesn't listen. Good thing her platelets are good, or it would never stop bleeding. All of Lucy's other numbers had crashed pretty low when we got them checked. We kind of expected them to. Her ANC was 1500 on Thursday last week, and was at 320 yesterday. Her white blood count was also down, but she takes a nightly chemo, 6MP, and that is what chemo is supposed to do. But, in order for her to get her next high dose Methotrexate and stay on the plan, she has to have an ANC of at least 500 and WBC of 1500. So, they took her off the 6MP totally to allow her numbers to recover. We will go to St. Joseph hospital on Sunday to get a blood test to ensure they are on the rise before driving back down to Memphis on Monday. They didn't want us to make a trip if her numbers weren't good enough.

Every phase of treatment is important for different reasons, and the phase we are in now is important to keep her in remission and to make sure there are no cancer cells "hiding." Darn pesky things. We need to make sure we stay on protocol because if she were to relapse in this phase, it would very hard to get her body to go back into remission because her body becomes "resistant," in a sense, to the chemo she has gotten. So it would take a different approach. We are not expecting any relapse, but still need to understand why it's important to ensure we stay on track.

Lucy did get blood yesterday. We figured she may have needed it. Her hemoglobin was down when we left Memphis and close to transfusion point. We always joke about her mood after she gets blood. Like Zach said one time after she got blood in Memphis, she was telling fart jokes. So he said, "Whoever gave that blood must have been silly." And yesterday, she was grumpy, so I said "That person must have been angry on the day they gave blood." In all honesty, we are grateful to those people that donate their blood.

So Zach is going into work today to get his assignments and talk to his manager. We will both be able to hopefully work every other week, or at least the week we are home. So part time is better than nothing. We were hoping we could work while in Memphis too, but we shall see. It's hard. It's a 24/7 operation taking care of Lucy in Memphis and keeping her entertained, even with two of us. Inpatient is a different world. Heck, it's hard to work with her at home, so you can imagine.

I also am feeling a need to get on that elliptical or start running again. Funny thing when a 3-year-old gets cancer, your immortality no longer exists. Now, I was nearing that age anyhow where you think "Huh, I really do need to take care of myself cuz I'm no spring chicken," but it hit even harder in the last few months. Plus, I think it would be a good stress reliever. Now, just to find time to get it in. And did I tell you that my husband weighs less than me???? That just isn't right!! Hahaha!! And Uncle Denny brought us cookies. And not just a dozen cookies... a tub FULL of them!!! UGH! Lucy can't have them due to her diet, so we don't give them to Jack because we don't want to cause that fight. So guess who eats them? Yep! me! LOL, damn cookies.....

Today, Zach is going to get the water situation rectified, hopefully. We have new filters coming in that we hope won't get plugged in a day. Then, he's going to get insulation for the attic. We needed to do this before this all happened. And both cars need brakes. UGH! Of course they do. At the same time. Then, I'll try to get out later and get my poor son some new clothes. He has apparently had a growth spurt! None of his jeans fit him, and his other pants are a little like he's waiting for a flood. Good thing I have him wear boots; you can hardly tell.

Day 55, Feb 18, 2011 6:13am
Yesterday was one of those busy days where you run around and do lots of stuff then at the end of the day you sit back and look around and say, "Wow, what did I do today???" There is absolutely no physical evidence that I did a damn thing. Staying

at home means cooking 3 meals and cleaning up 3 times. When I worked, I only had to do that once! And I didn't have to do the clean up! Zach did. Plus, keeping a 3-year-old entertained basically entails getting out different projects for her to do, then cleaning up after each one (rather directing her to clean up which takes much more time), and then starting all over.

Somebody said, "Yea! Today is Friday!" And I said, "Boo! that means only 3 more days left at home." At least Jack is out of school today and Monday, so the kids will get to spend all of that time together. Believe it or not, I prefer both kids at home, whereas before the cancer, we would split the kids when one had to run errands. I have found that since the cancer, they really must have learned a new appreciations for one another because they play wonderfully. I'm sure that will start to cease, but for now I'm enjoying it.

That and a conversation I had with somebody yesterday really got me thinking about a few things. My children have a new appreciation for something, but they don't know how to verbalize it, or even that they have to verbalize it. They have somehow understood the importance of one another and being home and being a family. And they are 5 and 3. At that age, the world revolves around them, especially the 3 year old. Jack is changing as he gets older to think more about others, but there is still that underlying psychological process that everything is related to something he has or hasn't done. So for them to "get" the idea to appreciate things more is a huge deal.

As adults, we always say "life is precious, don't waste a moment, etc.." We especially say it when something tragic happens to us or somebody around us, but within a few weeks or months, we are back at our old routine. And this is something we make a conscious effort to change. I wonder how I can become more like my children and start appreciating and living life differently without having to think about it all the time. And how do I make sure that I never stop doing this again?

It occurred to me (another thing I learned from Dale Carnegie--

seriously folks worth it to take the class) that in order to LIVE life like this, you have to make it a part of life and a habit. It's like retraining your brain -- a paradigm shift. I know I am getting all philosophical; sorry about that. I know I'm no Socrates with my words, but it is something that had a huge impact on me yesterday.

Another St. Jude mom sent me a poem about the things about cancer they want to keep. And going on that same thought and the idea that I don't want to wait for another tragedy to hit to think about living life to the fullest, here are the things about cancer I am grateful for and what cancer has made me realize:

1.   I get to spend every day with my little girl and more time with my son than I ever have before. I am with her 24/7, and that would not be the case if she didn't have cancer. I would be at work all day and then coming home at night. I would be consumed with "routine".

2.   Money is not the most important thing in this world. Dave Ramsey says that people always say "if I had lots of money, I could do this and that," and he says that if you did give those people money, they still wouldn't be happy. Money is a thing, not an emotion, but society has trained us to relate the two. I hope to never do that again. Money is a means of living our life, period.

3.   I always knew my husband was funny and wonderful, but I never realized how much I couldn't stand up without him, or rather how I DON'T want to stand up without him.

4.   For a moment during all the chaos in the beginning, I didn't care what anybody thought about me or their opinions of me; then as things started to get "normal", I went back to that self-criticism and worry. But just for a moment. I liked the other way better. That was a HUGE stressor for me and consumed so much of my day and time and has for most of my life: worrying about what others think and trying to ensure that everybody liked me. That is so unrealistic, I can't believe I would worry about it. This one will be a personal goal that I will definitely

have to remind myself of day in and day out until it becomes a habit.

5.   Home is not a place of stress or of chaos; it's a place of comfort.

6.   My son needs just as much attention as my daughter with cancer does. No, he's not having gasoline poured in his veins, but he is definitely having something poured into his heart and needs all of our attention. Last night, he showed me a journal of all the words he knows how to spell, and I didn't even know he knew them. How did I miss that? Shame on me.

7.   There are truly kind people in this world who want nothing more than to help others. Why was I such a cynic before? Cancer has taught me the graciousness of a stranger's heart and selflessness of their help. Man, I hope this one sticks. I don't want to go around thinking people are only doing things for their own selfish reasons; what a horrible paranoia to have.

Those are just a few things that stick out; things I don't think I would have ever realized if Lucy hadn't gotten cancer, so for those things, I am thankful.

I told you Lucy was destined for great things. The first being changing her mother's philosophy about some things in life. She won't understand this now, but I hope I can show her by raising her to be this way, and as an adult, she will never have to wait for a tragedy to hit to "live life to its fullest."

Day 56, Feb 19, 2011 6:56am
Ok, so let me tell you how our day went yesterday.......

6 am: Both children up and ready to go. Breakfast made for both, one wanted a granola bar, the other cereal in a cup (Lucy is the cereal in a cup girl)
6:10: First daily check of Lucy for a fever
6:30: Both children want something else to eat.
6:45: Children fighting over what to watch on TV. This happens every day. Lasts about 15 minutes until we just turn off the TV...

then they miraculously agree upon something.

7:00: Here comes the first round of items from their rooms into the living room. This day it was the tub of all their art stuff. They both have so much stuff that we had to buy them each a HUGE tub to put their things in.

7:15: Check Lucy for fever

8:00: I cleaned the kitchen for the FIRST time of the day and started a load of laundry.

9:00: Kids are hungry... granola bars and juice boxes.

9:15: Empty juice boxes and granola wrappers littered on the floor; I proceed to yell at said children to pick them up.

9:30: First load of laundry still going... water pressure is so low from the water system being filled with sediment, it takes a long time to go through. Can't do dishes or anything else while washer is running.

10:00: Kids are ready to get out a new activity, so I tell them they must clean up what they already have out.

10:45: I start making lunch and continue to tell kids to pick up their art stuff.

10:46: I check on kids progress of picking up stuff. Lucy apparently has painted her face, head, and hands. Nice. Good look for her.

11:30: Daddy gets home from hooking up the internet at his mom's house and proceeds to yell at children to PICK UP THEIR ART STUFF!!

11:45: Lunch is ready. Kids pick up art stuff within 5 minutes.

12:00: Lunch.

12:15: Check Lucy for fever.

12:30: Nap.

1:45: Lucy yelling from her room, "I'm ready to get up!"

1:46: Check Lucy for fever.

2:00: More art stuff comes flooding out of the room.

2:15: My uncle and aunt come over to assess the water situation and drop off a HEPA filter system.

2:30: I clean up lunch dishes.

3:00: Kids are again hungry.

3:30: I start a load of laundry... again no water pressure.

4:00: I start load of dishes... no water.

4:30: I start cooking dinner on the grill, and kids start cleaning up their mess. I say anything left on the floor goes in the garbage.

5:00: Dinner. Kids fighting at table over who is going to sit next to mom.

5:10: Check Lucy for fever.

5:30: Can finally finish the rinse cycle in the washing machine; clean the kitchen for the 3rd time of the day.

6:00: Zach tries to clean the bathroom... with no water...

6:30: I turn off washing machine so I can build up the water to give Lucy a bath.

6:45: Start filling up tub for Lucy's bath.

7:00: Tub is about 1/4 full for Lucy's bath, and I pop her in there.

7:15: Small amount of water is getting cold, so Lucy gets out of bath.

7:30: I fill up bath for Jack; he gets ready to get in with toys and is naked, only to find out... only cold water. No bath for him tonight.

7:45: Lucy and I watch Wizard of Oz, and she is very concerned about who is going to be performing the surgery to give the tin man, or robot as she calls him, a brain, and who will be doing the same for the scarecrow. Then she says, "How do you get courage? Do you eat it?"

8:30: Zach removes one of the filters from our water system to see if we can get some better water pressure. It works, but water coming out of faucet is brown... yuck!

9:00: Water clears a little, so I finish rinsing the 2nd load of laundry I put in. and then we put kids to bed, and check Lucy for fever.

9:15: I am dead to the world in my bed and sleep like a baby.

Day 57, Feb 20, 2011 7:28am

Yesterday, Zach and I were going stir crazy. The sun was out and it was so beautiful; we really were itching to get out of the house TOGETHER!! One of Zach's high school classmates bought us tickets to the Cash Bash in Lexington, and my good friend, Dana, came over to watch the kids for a few hours and it was AWESOME!!!

At first, we were very nervous to leave the house, and we weren't sure if it was because we were leaving Lucy for the first time, or if it was going out in the real world for the first time that triggered anxiety. I know I felt a little guilty for going to have some fun. I know we need to have time together, but there is still this little voice that says we should be with our little cancer patient 24/7. Once we got there, we relaxed and had an awesome time. We stayed for 4 hours, and it flew by so quick!

When we got home, Lucy looked at us as we walked in the door and said, "What are you doing home?" I am sure the break from us was nice for her too. They had a great time and suckered Dana into a few things. I said, "Is she suckering you into more food?" and Dana said, "Yea, it's hard to say no to a cancer patient." EXACTLY!!! Now somebody feels our pain! LOL, although, we are getting much better at it now.

For a moment last night, we were "normal". Then, everybody we saw asked how Lucy was doing and reality set in. Also, people think since she is in remission that we are done with treatment, and that is not the case. Leukemia is not like other cancers where you do treatment until you are in remission, then you are done. We do the 2.5 years of treatment regardless of her remission status. She will get chemo on a daily basis for the next 2 years. And then every week, she gets a stronger dose. It is the one thing that research has taught doctors: if you treat the disease consistently for 2.5 years, recurrence is less likely. And we definitely don't want recurrence because her body won't respond to the chemo as well, and it will be double doses or a bone marrow transplant, which for obvious reasons, we would like to avoid.

This morning, daddy and Lucy are going into OSF to get her blood work done. We need to check her numbers to make sure they are at acceptable levels so we can head to Memphis tomorrow to get her next spinal tap and high dose Methotrexate. We are hoping they are good; we don't want to sway from protocol at all. She's going to be pretty angry because they are doing a finger prick for the blood work. St. Jude told us not to let ANYBODY access her port except St. Jude personnel. Risk of infection is too high. So she'll be yelling at us later, I'm sure.

I'll post an update of numbers and if we head to Memphis tomorrow or not later...

CHAPTER 6
CONSOLIDATION & HIGH DOSE METHOTREXATE

Day 58, Feb 21, 2011 6:32am
Today is the day we head back down to Memphis. We will be splitting up the trip this time to make it easier on Lucy. Our plan is to drive to Marion, stay at a hotel, and then get up Tuesday morning and finish our drive.

For some reason, I had some major anxiety last night when I thinking about returning to Memphis. It brought up the exact same emotions I had when we first got her diagnosis. Actually, it started after Dr. Ross from Peoria St. Jude called with her numbers. All of her numbers seem to be a bit on the rise with the exception of her platelets that have dropped from 330,000 to 177,000 and her white blood count has dropped too. But they are still all within good range to travel and get procedure for now. We will get them tested again Tuesday night to double check.

That is the thing about her numbers... sometimes it's so nerve wracking when you get them and often there is no rhyme or reason because she has been off of all meds and chemo since last Tuesday, so not sure why they are dropping. The scary thing about the platelets is that was the first sign of cancer we had because they were low, so it always scares us when they drop thinking the cancer is back. But the doctors assure us that it's just her body and how it reacts to recovering. They say often, the other numbers will come up while the platelets drop, but eventually, they will rise too. She is still good in terms of transfusions. They usually transfuse below 50,000. When we first got to St. Jude they were like 20,000 or below, so I know 177,000 is ok.

I'm comforted by Memphis and St. Jude because it's the best place in the world, but at the same time it's like "Oh yea, she has cancer." Not that I ever really forget totally, but being home helps to remain normal... well, besides the fact that you have a bald child running around! Ha! Zach calls her uncle Fester! :)

So Zach and I got another opportunity to go out to dinner at Grand Cafe and go see True Grit. It was nice and relaxing. Just what we needed before we get in a car for a long journey with a very moody 3 year old! Ha! Cancer or no cancer, Lucy has never been a good traveler.

We have gotten most things packed, and I had to pack her food since her ANC is still at 520, and she can only have processed food. Do you know how hard it is to find some sort of processed food that is substantial as a meal for traveling? I mean, sure, there are tons of snacks, etc., but not a whole lot of substance. I guess if all else fails, we can go to a restaurant and explain we need it to go from frozen to cooked and handled with special care, but we aren't in that comfort zone yet. I know some parents do that and are comfortable with it. They go to McDonalds and explain that their child has leukemia and have to have fresh cooked food. Then the parents watch as they prepare it, and I hear that McDonalds is actually pretty good about it. So that, too, is an option.

I mentioned that Zach and I got out; Lucy was also ecstatic about us leaving for the last two nights for a couple of hours! I'm sure she is like "Get these people out of my face." Little grandma came over and watched them since she will be watching Jack all week anyhow, and she just stayed all night.

We are hoping to hit the road about noon and get to Marion at 4ish. That is where we will set up camp for the night, and then onward we go to Memphis Tuesday morning. We will settle in to the Grizzly House, where we will be staying this trip. The housing is set up based on your expected stay. 7 days or less is a stay at Grizzly, over 7 days is RMH, and long term stay is the Target house. Anyhow, after we get our things moved into Grizzly, we are going to go visit our "family" over at the RMH, and then we have to be at the hospital at 6 pm to get our bag of fluids to take back to the room with us.

So we are hoping only one day inpatient, and then they send us home on Friday or Saturday for another 9 day reprieve. We shall see....

Day 59, Feb 22, 2011 7:21am

We made it to our halfway point as planned yesterday and checked into a Hampton Inn. Lucy was hungry when we got here, and we were debating if we should have her eat the Chef Boyardee I packed, or if we should go out to a restaurant. Her numbers were barely over the acceptable limit for going out on Sunday, but she kept saying she was STARVING! LOL! Even though I kept her filled with snacks for the entire 4 hour car trip! We decided to go ahead and go out. The waitress was very accommodating. We asked for fresh only and no seasoning. Lucy got a chicken breast and mac n' cheese that is prepackaged and cooked individually. We always make Lucy wear a mask when she isn't eating... this time of year, I'm not risking it!! Anyhow, Zach had asked if I had heard the guy next to us, and thank goodness I hadn't!!

Apparently, he was going off that Lucy shouldn't be allowed in the restaurant if she was going to be giving him something contagious. What an asshole. If I had heard, I wouldn't have been so nice! As he was paying, I did see him point to us and our waitress was talking to him, so she was telling him she has cancer. Hope it made him feel like shit.

When we were done eating, we had Lucy put her mask on again before we left. We were walking out the front door and a nice lady was holding the door. First, Zach went, then here came me and Lucy. She wasn't so nice anymore! Let go of that door and practically shut it! I know people see a mask and think she may be contagious, but really? A little girl with no hair and you're afraid for your safety?

And you know the funny thing? As Lucy was eating, she said, "Why aren't people staring at me and seeing my Beatles shirt?" Hahaha! Little did she know that they were, but not for her shirt. I love her!!

So I got to sleep with little miss bed hog last night... just like her dad!! Today, we will finish our trek to Memphis! First stop... RMH!!

Day 60, Feb 23, 2011 6:26am

Well, we got all settled in last night and were very fortunate to be able to stay at the RMH! Yea!! Not that the Grizzly House is bad, but here there are kitchens to prepare food, friends, and activities for Lucy to do. Plus, they don't call it "the house that love built" for any old reason!! We truly feel "at home." The only thing I wish is that I could run home and scoop Jack up!

Last night when we took Lucy over to the hospital to get her fluids, we walked in and that "smell" hit me right away. It's that clean hospital smell. And for the oddest reason, it's like I exhaled. Comfort, familiarity, and self-assurance all came flooding back. And last night as I was unpacking our things in our room, I wished I could just set up the temporary housing and always have a room here. Here, Lucy goes in for a spinal tap and inpatient for her high dose chemo, and I'm less stressed than I was at home. That should give you an idea of how wonderful St. Jude is if you hadn't figured it out yet. ;)

Today, we see Pui at 9:30, procedure at 10:30, and then we get admitted after that. Definitely going to try something different this time for drugs to knock her out in the hopes she wakes up not so grumpy and doesn't throw up. Also hoping we don't have to wait for a room for hours like last time. I would like to just get her admitted and get the nasty chemo started. Quicker we start, quicker we are done! This time, as long as she is clearing the Methotrexate well, we only stay inpatient 24 hours. So we keep telling her, you have to drink and pee a lot!!

So, think positive thoughts and wish for lots of pee today!! Ha! Will update after procedure to let you all know how she did. Always hate when she has to go under. Nerve wracking.

Day 61, Feb 24, 2011 7:20am

Last night went well after Lucy wasn't so mad about having to stay inpatient. I don't think she realized it until later, and then she was angry. But daddy gave her some snacks and put in Wizard of Oz and all was good. We also tried to get her to watch American

Idol last night since it was all Beatles songs. She was not impressed! Hahaha, she made daddy turn it off. Perhaps, she should have been a judge!

I stayed with Lucy last night at the hospital and got to sleep on the ever-so-uncomfortable couch. But, I slept most of the night, waking a few times when they came to check her urine and getting blood. She slept like a champ!

Will wait to see how her body is processing the Methotrexate, and we will likely get to go back to the RMH this evening then come back tomorrow for lab work.

Day 63, Feb 26, 2011 6:03am
Wow!! We have been so busy that I have been too exhausted to post at night and actually sleeping in a bit in the morning. Lucy was released from the hospital on Thursday evening around 8:30. It was a crazy discharge of tornado warnings happening while we were trying to leave. There were apparently a few touchdowns all around the area. Zach, Lucy, and I went to the basement. All other inpatients were moved to the middle of the floor. It was funny because we were the only three people in the basement and were joking that we were from Illinois and always go to basements for tornados, so these people must be used to warnings if they stay on the floors doing their business. Kind of like we are used to snow; they are used to twisters....huh...

And our night of excitement didn't end there!! We lost our truck keys and were trying to either find them or figure out how to get new ones made. I searched the dark parking lot in a downpour and had no luck. We opted to come back to the RMH via shuttle and make some calls. You know the automatic locks you have on your key ring?? And that "feature"? Let's just say unless you want to be set back a couple hundred dollars, don't lose your keys!! As we got back here and were making phone calls to see who was the cheapest, a wonderful nurse named "Jenny" called and said she found our keys!! Woo hoo!!! Thanks Jenny! Don't know who you are, but a big shout out to you!!!

Lucy came back to the RMH on fluids to help clear the rest of the Methotrexate she still had in her system, and we were to return to the hospital at noon yesterday to check her levels and see if she could go off fluids and be discharged. I took her over to the hospital while Zach was here getting fitted for a tux. Her numbers looked good, so we were able to take her off fluids and even de-access her port all together. Let me tell you while she is hooked up to a bag of fluids, it really is a pain in the butt! Carrying a bag all over and reminding her not to step on her wires is a full time job! Plus, it really limits what she can do.

Oh, so I mentioned Zach was fitted for a tux!! And after I got back from the hospital, I got to go shopping for a gown!!! Why?? Because we have been asked to attend "Oscars night" here in Memphis to help raise money for the Ronald McDonald house. Oscars night is one of the few private viewings of the Oscars live that is sanctioned by the Academy. The affiliate stations are present and there are silent and live auctions held to raise money for the House. Three families were chosen to talk about our story and what the RMH means to us. They pay for our beautiful dresses and tux, and Lucy gets to go shopping today for a beautiful gown. They pick us up in a limo! And we get to attend this red carpet affair with music, food, drinks, and of course the Oscars! They say that it may get national coverage; it does sometimes. So set your DVRs on Sunday during the Oscars in case Lucy is on the big screen! And even if it doesn't, we are helping to raise money for an awesome cause.

Last night I went shopping with the other moms to Dillard's who donated our clothes along with one of the patients who is 15 years old, Amber, and has become close with Lucy. I haven't shopped like that in a long time. Then we went out for dinner afterwards. One mom has been here for 7 years with her son Timmy. He has had a brain tumor 3 different times over the 7 years, and now he has multiple tumors and they are all in his spinal cord as well. She was so excited to get out, as she should be. It was nice to laugh and joke with these women.

So today, Lucy gets to go to this boutique and pick out her dress.

She's excited!! She said she wants pink!! Of course she does. ;) She will be even more excited when she gets picked up by a limo and gets to actually leave the house! She hasn't been anywhere except for home, here, and the hospital since x-mas. We will take her mask, but we're hoping to let her dance with it off for a little bit since her counts weren't too bad when they checked them yesterday. I wish Jack were here. But Zach said, "Well, since you are always into fairness and like to keep it "even" between the kids, Jack got to go to the benefit and Lucy didn't," so that helps me not feel so bad... plus, Jack gets to leave the house, and Lucy rarely does.

So today we get her dress, and tomorrow we party! Woo hoo!! I can't wait to see Zach in a tux. I haven't seen that since our wedding, and he was mighty handsome then! We will head back to Illinois on Monday instead of today, so we are delayed a bit in getting home, but we really couldn't pass up the opportunity for Lucy and to express our gratitude to the RMH. I'll take lots of pics and video too!!

Day 64, Feb 27, 2011 8:13am
Ok, so I tried to do this update once and my netbook rebooted in the middle of it, so I have to start again...grrr. LOL!

Tonight is our last night at the RMH; we will head home tomorrow and split the trip up again. We will be home-home by Tuesday. I'm excited to see Jack; I miss him to pieces, but we are going to make our last night here a fabulous one!! Lucy is so excited about "the Ball" as she calls it. She says she is Snow White, I am Belle, and daddy is Prince Charming.

Yesterday, she got to go shopping for her clothes and it was the BEST day ever. It was also the first time she has been out of the house to do something other than go to the hospital. Our first stop was a wonderful children's boutique called Cotton Tails. What a wonderful place. The clothes were beyond gorgeous and the staff was fantastic with her. Have you ever seen Pretty Woman when Julia Roberts goes to the department store, and she has a woman helping her with clothes, another with shoes, and yet another for accessories? That was Lucy yesterday.

She fell in love with the first dress she tried on, as did I. It was pink and sparkly! Of course, when we first walked into the store, she gravitated straight to the shoes! LOL! We told her we would do shoes last. What a true woman... already in love with shoes.

So she was twirling in her dress and got a new headband that was absolutely gorgeous, then we moved to shoes. She had said the night before that she wanted shoes just like mine, only a different color. I had gotten black patent Mary Janes. So, when the lady pulled out the Mary Janes for her to try on, she was sold!

Only she didn't just stop there; she had to try on every last pair first! Zach said, "Just like a woman, already know which ones you want, but still have to try on every damn pair." She LOVES the shoes. She says they sound so tappy! Hahah! When we were in ballet, she eyed the tap shoes all the time asking when she got to get those. So she says now she has a pair of tap shoes. The boutique donated all her clothing, undergarments, shoes, and accessories. They were AWESOME. They also posted pictures of her on their webpage aftewards. Check them out at http://www.cotton-tails.com/ to see her picture! The shop owner, Micki, also gave us a good place to get Baby White a new outfit, handed us an envelope, and told us she would like to pay for the dolls clothes and buy us lunch. What wonderful generosity from a stranger. We felt so humbled.

So off to lunch at Chili's we went. This is the first time Lucy has been out since before the cancer in December. So she was thrilled to have time away from hospitals. At lunch, we told the waiter to please not season her food and definitely no pepper. When we got her food, there was pepper on her fries and seasoning on her chicken.. Zach looked at the waiter and said, "Is that pepper?", the waiter rolled his eyes and walked off. Zach was mad, as was I. Really? We told him she had cancer, and that is something she CANNOT have. So we had to take her fries away. Who puts pepper on fries? Apparently, Chili's.

After we left lunch, we went to the toy store and got White a beautiful pink dress to match Lucy's. Lucy was excited. After that, we walked into a nearby salon and asked if they could shave Lucy's head. It was growing back unevenly and only in the back, so we wanted to even it up. The shop was busy and had a long line of patrons waiting, so we didn't expect to get a seat. But they were awesome and took her right away. She had a blast sitting in her chair getting all ready for night out.

After that, we headed back to the RMH for a much needed nap! Lucy passed out before we got back, she was so exhausted. When she woke up from nap, the first thing she wanted to do was wear her shoes! LOL!
Tonight, we are being picked up at 5:45 by a limo to take us to the red carpet affair. I will be sure to take lots of pictures and video too. Let's see if we can keep Lucy out of her dress until then!!! :)

Day 66, Mar 1, 2011 7:31am
We are on our way home-home and when we get there later today, I will upload pics from the Oscar party and tell you all about how Lucy was definitely the show stopper!!!

Day 67, Mar 2, 2011 8:56am
Wow, sometimes I think being home is even crazier than being in Memphis. In Memphis, you just worry about two things: Lucy and chemotherapy. Here, you have a whole new level of stress. House, dog, bills, work, son, car, water, and cleaning....UGH. I'm not complaining too much because I LOVE being home. I love Taco and my bed and my couch; I even love our duct tape chair. We have had this chair forever... got it from Zach's mom, and it's so old, but SOO comfy. We just re-upholster with duct tape when needed.

So yesterday was nice, hearing my children playing and screaming and laughing. It never gets old. Jack is so proud, he tells everybody about "his sister." Even when he is talking to us, he will say "That is my sister's." He said he could hardly sit still at school because he wanted us to be home. And of course, Lucy talks about her "brudder." :) We are so lucky to have two wonderful, caring children.

Since it has been a few days since I posted, I'll attempt to cover all the wonderful and amazing things that have happened to us since Sunday.

Who would have thought cancer would have brought us some wonderful things? We have learned a whole new side of mankind and are a little embarrassed that we had little faith in it prior. It's like those end of the world shows, you know the ones... "The Road", "Eli", etc. where it shows how people are horribly corrupt and take full advantage of one another. And it shows survival mode kicking in and people only caring for themselves. I always said that I didn't think if something catastrophic happened, the world would end up that way. Maybe I am naive, but after this experience, I believe that even more so. I don't think people are only motivated by power and greed.

In college, my major was political science, so philosophy was a very strong part of my curriculum. Nietzsche was probably one of my favorites. Unfortunately, sometimes people associate his thinking with Hitler because Hitler based his ruling off of how HE interpreted Nietzsche. Anyhow, he always said that power is what motivated people and that power didn't necessarily have to be evil or be power in the sense of leading people. I can see that power is the power to help others, feel good about oneself, and power over circumstance. Others may interpret it differently, but I can tell you first hand, I have seen something like that in the last 3 months we have been dealing with cancer. People are amazing, and even when we run into those who aren't so fabulous, the two we meet later always make up for that. Anyhow, my point is: if the world were to come to a catastrophic end and few were to survive, I vote that people would rally together rather than fight like dogs.

Case in point: We stopped at Steak n Shake in Marion, Il yesterday. That is our half-way point and our home base when traveling with Lucy. A lady came up and asked Lucy what her name was; then she looked at me and said, "Hey, I remember you." I had stopped there before to eat during one of my trips with Jack and during one of my solo trips. I had a Team Lucy shirt on and she had inquired about her. Anyhow, she looked at us and said, "I have been praying for you, Lucy, and would like to buy your dinner." We were stunned and humbled. I don't know how to explain it any other way. We always feel like saying, "No, that's ok, thank you very much" because we feel bad. Then, somebody reminded me once that people like to help and feel good about doing something, and I always remember that and say "Thank you."

So the lady bought our dinner, and then comes over and hands Lucy an envelope with all her tips from the day. We didn't know what to say or do? She also handed her two stuffed animals and told us that from now on our meals are free there and that she had already talked to the manager. I met this lady twice before and here she has done a wonderful thing for us. It gets costly going back and forth to Memphis every other week and having to stop at a hotel twice during the trip. And here she has made it more manageable by giving us a free meal. Absolutely amazing.

And that isn't all the generosity we encountered. Sunday was our trip to the Oscar party to raise money for the RMH. Besides all the stores providing us with free clothes, the overwhelming feeling of love and acceptance was awesome.

We were a little worried that day that we were not going to make it to the party. Lucy woke up and wasn't feeling the greatest. She slept all morning, which isn't like her, and her temp was 99.9... so on the verge of hospital stay. We let her rest and hoped it was just the side effects of the daily oral chemo she gets; it really puts her down. She woke up around 2 in the afternoon, and the first thing she said was "Is it time to put on my tappy shoes?" We knew she was feeling better! First thing I did was paint her fingernails and toenails. She was saying "This takes so long to dry."

Daddy told her that was part of being a girl: waiting for polish to dry and wearing shoes that weren't always comfortable but looked great. Gotta love him, he really does pay attention. ;) So we got all dressed up, and then we went out to the front lobby for pictures. Everybody looked AMAZING! Then they told us our limo was there, so we told Lucy our car was here. She walked out the door, and the shuttle to the hospital was out front, so she proceeded to get on. We told her, "Oh honey, your car is behind the shuttle and its MUCH nicer." She saw that limo and didn't know what to think. She loved it!! Jack says, "that's what fancy people ride in.". Hahaha!

When we got to the party, we got to walk a red carpet, and of course everybody oohed and ahed over Lucy. She did look pretty sweet. :) There were food vendors set up all around with amazing gourmet food. and there were bars set up for drinks. It was nice to have a few "adult" drinks and relax. Lucy loved the crepe booth they had set up.

Then the band started to play, and she was on that dance floor in no time. The ONLY one on the dance floor too! She didn't care. Of course Miss Debbie from RMH was out there with her. Within in no time, the band had her on stage dancing and singing. At one point, they were singing a song to her. That freaked her out! LOL! They had her sitting on this chair in the middle of the stage and it looked as if she might cry. After that, she laid off dancing for a while! But in no time, she was back out there.

Then they did the live auctions and asked the family to be on stage and say a few things prior. We talked about our experience at the RMH, and then Lucy also had a few words to say. ;) She did so good at answering questions, and talking in that microphone was like second nature to her. Also being on stage and twirling in her dress was second nature.

We were up there for quite some time, so she got restless and was running back and forth while the auction was going on, and we had to lay down the law and take her backstage, and she screamed at the top of her lungs...awesome.

The band was also backstage so she got to talk to them and, of course, was a ham. Then later in the evening, she got back on the dance floor and was dancing with everybody there. She also started getting brave and just walking up on the stage on her own and dancing when she felt like it! LOL! We knew it was time to go when she went to sit on one of the RMH manager's lap and was about crashed. She also got to use Miss Debbie's camera and was snapping pictures all night long. Can't wait to see what she got!!!

And seeing Zach in a tux and dancing with him was awesome. It was nice to get out and have fun and laugh. Zach doesn't think he's a good dancer, but I think he does a fabulous job of twirling me on the dance floor. He makes me feel so elegant and special. I had a smile on my face the entire time we were dancing. We left in the limo, and she went home and crashed. I would say that she had a BLAST at her "ball."

The next morning, we got up and started packing, and we noticed a sore on Lucy's mouth. We thought "crap!" So we called the hospital and they wanted to see her. If her numbers get too low, the sores can present a real problem. We were worried that we weren't going to be able to go home after all. We spent most of Monday at the hospital getting tests and blood work. They all came out ok, and her ANC was 800 which was good enough for travel. If they hit below 500, there is no travel allowed. Zach said, "Well, it's like we had too much fun the night before and now we are being punished." Ha! It was really more like we were able to step out of reality for a moment, and then the next day we were reminded that cancer waits for nothing.

So today is day one of our 6 days here at home. Hope to get the water situation FINALLY figured out. Then we may have to look at getting a new vehicle. :(Our Saturn Vue has always given us electrical problems since day one of buying it, and unfortunately, we weren't quick enough to turn it in for the Lemon Law by like one week. UGH. THEN Saturn goes out of business. Anyhow, the brakes aren't working so fabulously anymore due to electrical problems, the cruise control decides to go out on a whim, and the cost to repair isn't worth it since we have already had this problem before and gotten it "fixed." It's not fixed if it keeps happening, and we have 2.5 years of trips and need a reliable vehicle if we are carrying precious cargo. Totally stinks, but we are going to try to look at options while we are home. Plus, we are both going to try to work and pull a partial paycheck. I think we can make it happen. :)

This phase of treatment is just so hectic since we are back and forth every other week and travel is a full 4 days with having to split it up. Lucy has chemo that just doesn't agree with her, so long car rides aren't possible. There is a train that goes from Champaign to Memphis at night, but that's when she gets chemo, so it would make her too sick to be in a moving vehicle. And flying is too expensive since we can't book it in advance, not knowing her numbers. After this phase is over, things will settle down, and we will be doing weekly visits to Peoria and only going to Memphis about every 8 weeks. We have two high dose Methotrexates down! Only two more to go. We can do it.

Day 69, Mar 4, 2011 6:19am
Today is Zach and my 5 year anniversary! Holy cow... time flies when you have a house, a dog, 2 kids, and cancer. We get to celebrate tonight with dinner at Desthil! I'm so excited. We are going to get all dressed up and use our duds from the Oscar party, since we probably won't have anywhere else to wear them, and I asked a friend to take pictures of us since we didn't get any good ones of the two of us that night. It'll be just like prom! Ha!

We got the water situation figured out (we hope and think). We are waiting on parts to arrive, then my uncle is going to put it all together while we are in Tennessee for Lucy's treatment next week. That will be nice to be able to feel comfortable giving Lucy a bath without worrying. We also went looking at some vehicles and found a few models we may be interested in. Now we are just doing some research as to prices and best places to purchase from. We are trying to use negotiating tricks we learned in our Dave Ramsey class! Let's see how well we do. I'm usually not good at that sort of thing. I would be a horrible poker player.

Lucy is doing good besides two new sores on the outside of her lip… actually more on her chin. She keeps biting her bottom lip, and it is making her chin irritated. I keep putting ointment on it, so hopefully with her numbers so low it won't turn into an infection. And of course she is acting like a 3-year-old again, and if you have a 3-year-old or have ever had one, you understand what I am talking about. She is sassy, talks back, is defiant, wants to be independent on things she wants, and otherwise wants us to wait on her hand and foot… the fits she throws are lovely, and the sticking her tongue out at us is even better! Ha! Glad to see her spunkiness come alive. Now we have to punish her for some of it. Time out is ineffective because she has been in virtual time out for 3 months. No spankings or swats because, well, she has cancer. Hahahaha! :) Can't really take anything away from her; she doesn't seem to care. She has been without toys before, so she has learned to use her imagination better without them. I have resorted to a spot on the wall where she has to stand and put her nose up against it. She hates it, so that is effective.

The nurses at St. Jude warned us that if we didn't still discipline then she would be a little terror, so we are trying to do something. 3-year-olds are worse than 2-year-olds; I don't care what anybody says.

Her numbers that came back were a little on the low side, so we have stopped the 6MP nightly chemo and will go in for a blood work-up on Sunday to ensure they are high enough to head back down to Memphis for our next high dose Methotrexate.

So until Sunday….. oh and can I say…Illinois weather really stinks?! After being in Memphis, I want 70 degrees back!!!

Day 71, Mar 6, 2011 6:11am
Today is our last full day home before heading back to Memphis tomorrow. Well, if Lucy's numbers are good we will head down. She will go into St. Joe this morning and get a finger prick to run a CBC differential like last time. Only this time will be worse because she will fully understand what is about to happen to her.

Zach and I were a little stressed out last night over all the stuff that we still need to get done before leaving. This trip home was a little shorter by three days, and we had an anniversary celebration to fit in there. It will be nice to have more than a week at home in between trips. This time we didn't unpack any of Lucy's stuff, so at least we don't have to pack again for her. We are planning on heading out around noon tomorrow so we can be in Marion, IL to stop for the night around 5 pm. Then finish the trip Tuesday and arrive at St. Jude as normal.

Zach and I were talking about the day she was diagnosed last night, and I found that is something I cannot discuss without getting sick to my stomach. I don't know why that has such an impact on me or makes me so nauseous, but it does. I mean, I don't know if it is the possibility of what could have happened had we not taken her to the ER or just the raw emotions I obviously still have over this whole ordeal. It's almost like sometimes I forget the gravity of the situation because she is doing so well, and then when I think of that day, it all comes pouring back.

Zach said he has a problem looking at old pictures of her. It makes him pretty upset, and I would have to agree with that statement. It's not just that she has lost her hair; it's that, for a while, even her facial expressions, attitude, and voice had changed. It's like looking at a different life. It is all slowly coming back now, though. That spirit I referenced in a journal post earlier… that is returning. I can see it in her smile and her actions. She is dancing a lot more now; still, some of it isn't 100% there, and I can't wait for it to return. She needs her friends to play with and a break from us! I can't wait till her numbers are high enough for her to play with her friends and other children.

So today we try to get as many things as possible crossed off our to-do list, take Lucy in to the hospital, work on a class project with Jack that isn't due until the following week, but we never know how long our trip to Memphis will last, and we need to pack.

I feel bad for Jack. Last night he was up for a while stressing out over who was going to stay with him when we go back to

Memphis. Poor kid. He is such a high-stress little boy, just like his mama. :(Too bad I had to give him that trait. When we get all through with the high dose Methotrexate, I will be setting up some therapy sessions for him. I tried to do it before, but a parent must be present, and we couldn't guarantee we would be there during this phase.

Man, this post kind of turned out to be a little bit of a Debbie downer... didn't mean for that to happen. Just reality. Good days, bad days. And it's not that yesterday was a "bad" day; just one of those where reality sets in a little bit harder than the day before. That is the other odd thing; you never know what is going to set it off. It is usually the smallest things.

I will update later about her numbers.

Day 71, Mar 6, 2011 7:35pm
Lucy's numbers are good... so good we are starting her nightly chemo tonight, which makes her so sick to her stomach. Anyhow, to Memphis we go! Leave around noon tomorrow, arrive in Marion, IL for a hotel to break the trip up, then leave Tuesday morning and check into St. Jude Tuesday night to get ready for procedure. Wednesday, we will go inpatient and hopefully be released Thursday evening! Home by Saturday!!! Hope, hope, hope!!!

Day 73, Mar 9, 2011 7:18am
Well, today is procedure day. Kind of nervous about this one, and I have no idea what it is that is making me on edge. This whole trip has been a little "edgy." I think it's just the fact that after you're home for a while and getting used to normal, it's a real kick to come back down here.

Yesterday, we went to check in at the Memphis Grizzly House since this stay is only supposed to be about 4 days. As we checked in, they were full so we got to come stay at the RMH again which we are very thankful for. We really love this place. We went to the side of the building that we had the very first time we stayed here, right after we got to Memphis, and when I walked in that room, something kicked me in the gut.

It's like when you smell something familiar, and it brings back a floodgate of memories. It wasn't the smell, but just looking at the room, which is identical to the first one we had. Sadness and fear and uncertainty was what I felt. Plus, it doesn't help that there is a solemn atmosphere around here due to another child who isn't doing so well.

This little boy was sent home last Thanksgiving, cancer free from a solid tumor only to have it come back fast and furious. So much so that despite chemo, it's growing. It's intertwined with his blood flow system behind his ear and wrapped with his nerves, so surgery is not an option. They said yesterday that he could die on the table if they did radiation, so that's not a possibility either. His mom said the doctors told her he shouldn't be walking or talking and have no idea how he's still so active. He is going to die. His name is Brayden, and he is six years old.

Reality. That's what's so tough about this place. And worry. Worry that a slight change in Lucy's numbers means the cancer is back. We hope not and have been reassured her number jump is normal, but after living through Braydens story, still worrisome.

Lucy's procedure is today. We hope to get a room early and start the Methotrexate early so we can be done early. I will post an update when she is out of surgery.

Day 73, Mar 9, 2011 5:50pm
Lucy came out of procedure ok. Still has vertigo and a little bit of anger. She did throw up this time. Still don't have her cocktail quite right. Plus, they woke her up way too early this time. I guess we just keep trying different things until we get it right.

She's doing good now though and sitting in her hospital bed eating Cheerios and watching Disney! Methotrexate has started and will run until approximately 5:15 tomorrow evening. Hopefully, her kidneys will clear the drug, and we will get to go back to RMH on fluids for another night.

Day 74, Mar 10, 2011 6:51am

Boy, I sure hope I get a nap today! Plastic couch sleeping, as we refer to sleeping at the hospital, is little to be desired! Especially when you've got a nurse coming into Lucy's room every two hours to make her go potty. I sure hope she's clearing that Methotrexate so we can sleep at RMH tonight.

At least the coffee in the break room is thick as mud. That should help!

Lucy crashed last night in about 5 minute's time. She had a long and busy day! Spinal tap, spinal injection of chemo, oral chemo, and chemo through her port. Then, a volunteer came and sat with her while Zach and I had a 30 minute date. It was awesome. We just walked around the hospital talking and laughing. Strange that we had a good time together in the hospital. We definitely have gotten to hang out more since this cancer started, and we realized last night that we truly are best friends. Sometimes in the hustle and bustle of life, you forget that or lose that.

After the volunteer left, we took Lucy down to the juke box area where they were doing arts and crafts. We stayed there for about 45 minutes, listening to the Beatles on the juke box and she got to paint. Then we took her back to the room, cleaned her up, and she crashed in no time!

Of course, the nurses were all over her the entire time. They say they are just in love with her and can't believe she's only 3 because of her conversations and how well she talks. I guess we always have talked to her like an adult and having Jack as an older brother who guides her has definitely helped to shape and mold her as well. Speaking of Jack, he was talking last night about how much he loves Lucy and misses us. He even said he was going to change his favorite color to pink because it was Lucy's favorite. For a 5-year-old boy, that is a big deal!!! He's so sweet and compassionate. I have the two most amazing children.

We found out yesterday how the next phase of treatment will go.

A week after her last high dose of Methotrexate, which starts March 23rd, we go into Continuation, or maintenance. It's the final phase and lasts 120 weeks.

Weeks 1-6, through the first week of May, we are home the entire time going to Peoria once a week for treatment. We don't have the exact plan yet, but she will get a mix of chemo pushes and be on a daily oral chemo. We also start another steroid called Dex. It's far worse than the Prednisone in terms of her behavior and outbursts, so definitely not looking forward to that! Ha! She's on it for 4 days then off for 3. Can't wait to see how chubby she's gonna get cuz I hear the food cravings are way worse.

Weeks 7-10, we do our Reinduction 1. We do this primarily in Memphis, so we will be gone pretty much the entire month of May. This is a treatment plan similar to when we first got to Memphis, so pretty intense. Then we come back home and continue what we did the first 6 weeks.

Then weeks 17-20, we are again in Memphis for Reinduction 2. Again, tough plan of lots of nasty chemo. That will be around the middle of July, through the first two weeks of August.

Then, for the remainder of the 2 years, we do weekly treatments at Peoria, daily chemo by mouth, and trips to St. Jude every 8 weeks. So we have a long, long road ahead of us, but at least most of it is at home! Well, I think I'll go grab another cup of that mud and hope for a nap today!!

Day 75, Mar 11, 2011 8:18am
Well, we got to come back to RMH last night on fluids! So, while the double bed was small, it was way better than the plastic couch. Lucy is doing well, and today we go in around 11 to make sure her body is clearing the Methotrexate. If it is, we are homebound this afternoon. We really wish we could do the whole drive in one shot, but Lucy, with or without chemo, is a bad traveler! Even with video games and movies! So hope for good numbers!!

Day 77, Mar 13, 2011 8:05am
We are home-home for 9 days. We had a hell of a long day at the hospital on Friday and then headed out. As we got on the road and saw Lucy was doing pretty good, we decided to just push on through and drive through the night instead of staying at a hotel. She did fine until she finally fell asleep. Then she woke up every 30 minutes or so, just mad at the world... and who could blame her? Those car seats were not made for comfort. She was tired, uncomfortable, and just wanted to lay down. We ended up pulling into home around 1:30 am Saturday, and she was happy to be in bed!

Friday was so stressful as Jack had an accident at school, and we weren't able to be home to take him to the ER. He was sliding down the fireman's pole and hurt his foot really bad. It swelled and he wasn't able to walk. I had my sister take him to the ER to ensure it wasn't broken. The x-rays came back that it wasn't broken, but they found something weird with his foot bone. UGH. He has some sort of bony structure growing in his soft tissue. We have no idea what that means. We are taking him to an orthopedic doctor on Monday. Of course our first thoughts go to the worst possible thing... cancer. And when you are staying in Memphis, it's hard to not have that type of thinking. You hear the weirdest kinds of cancer and ways that people found out, so while we are really trying to just think it's something odd he was born with, its putting a toll on our emotions. It is probably everything we have had built up for the past 3 months and the worry is just manifesting itself over the smallest situation.

The foot is still swollen, he cannot walk on it or put any pressure on it at all. Plus, there is the guilt for not being able to take him to the ER when he needed us most. At least we are done going to Memphis without him, so this situation hopefully won't ever present itself again.

All the books I have been reading talk about this sibling guilt and how parents deal with it. Zach and I have a huge amount of guilt as to what this is doing to Jack and how it's affecting his emotional state. The poor kid cries over everything, and I mean

EVERYTHING. And then he sat and watched his sister get all kinds of pokes when she went to the ER on that day of diagnosis, so he's scared to death that is going to happen to him over this foot deal. I know that some people will say we are making a big deal over it, and it's just a common foot issue, but when you take your child to the ER to be treated for strep, and she has cancer, you tend to go down that path more often. Plus, I think we are just so overwhelmed being home.

We have so much to do and 9 days to do it...well, 7 since we are leaving for Memphis early next trip and taking the kids to the zoo and downtown. It's Jack's spring break, so we are going to try to get in a few attractions so he doesn't have to say that he spent his spring break at St. Jude hospital while his sister got chemo! Ha!

We did get ALL of the water system finally delivered! It should be installed Wednesday. It's going to take up the entire area of our washer/dryer, so we no longer will have space for a dryer. Hmm....too bad it wasn't warm enough to hang clothes on the line. We have been researching stackable washer/dryers and looking at options like putting them in the garage. We shall figure it out.

Today, we will just start marking off to-do items one at a time and see how far we get by end of week. Jack is "featured friend" at school so Zach and I are taking turns going to school and eating lunch with him. Then he has an orthopedic appointment on Monday. Wednesday, Lucy has clinic in Peoria, Friday is 1/2 day school for Jack, and we have to go to work in between all this stuff. I'm so happy she only has one more Methotrexate treatment, then we will be home for 7 weeks straight! We welcome the break. While we still have to do treatment in Peoria, at least its once a week and close to home.

Well, I guess I better drink my coffee and finish up that to-do list... and for those of you wondering... Zach was good and did not tell Jack to rub some dirt on his foot. ;) He thought we should let the medical professionals take a look first... then, maybe...

Day 78, Mar 14, 2011 5:42am

24 hours in a day... Do you find that sometimes 25 or 26 hours would be awesome and much needed? Me too! And then to lose an hour! I would like to retaliate against Mother Nature and whoever invented daylight savings and get my hour back, please!! What would I do with that hour? Well, today I would use it to sleep!!

Anybody with small children understands how screwed up kids are for the entire week of a time change. And I see a full moon approaching on Friday... So, I would take my extra hour save it for Friday and sleep when the kids are going all nutso during the full moon!! Usually, the fits start around Wednesday evening, and get they get progressively worse by Thursday with mood swings, then finally by Friday, it's so out of hand, you say "Is it a full moon???" and yep! it usually is. I'm convinced that whoever wrote the first stories about werewolves were talking about their children! The legendary stories were passed down from parent to parent and, like the telephone game, got progressively more detailed and changed in form until the person who wrote it forgot that it was really talking all about children! All I can say is thank goodness Lucy is NOT on a steroid during this week! Or else I would move out and take up residence in a hotel room that had a Jacuzzi tub, bar, and room service.

Miraculously, last night before bed, Jack was able to put some pressure on his foot and walk! I wonder now if he's been messing with us. So, today he will be going to school this morning and to a doc appointment this afternoon. I am nervous and anxious to figure out exactly what this extra bone thing really means.

I am going to go to the laundromat as well sometime today. We just have too much to do, and with our water still being nasty, I cannot stand the way they smell even after they are clean. So, I'm going to take garbage bags of all the bedding and clothes and wash them in clean water. We also have to get ahead of the laundry since after Wednesday we will have no dryer due to the water system taking up our entire mud room. But I'm not complaining; I'm excited for clean water that doesn't have an odor! And Lucy can take a bath!! Yea!!

Okay, well I didn't really have any updates today... I just felt the need to rant about the loss of an hour and the full moon! Ha! I feel much better now...

Day 79, Mar 15, 2011 6:19pm
Odieharris.

Look up that Caringbridge site. It's a good friend we met while in Memphis, and right now their family could use all the thoughts, prayers, and positive thinking you can give them. Odie's mom had to make a difficult decision today to fulfill her son's wish. From one mom to another, my heart is breaking for her.

Day 80, Mar 16, 2011 6:48am
Today is our clinic day in Peoria. Hopefully, it will be just a quick blood draw and nothing more. If I had to judge by the way Lucy has been acting lately, I would say her numbers were good. But then again, sometimes they come back and surprise you!

Last night we put the kids to bed around 8:15, which is their normal time. Jack was out like a light. Lucy... well Lucy partied for some time in her room. We heard her talking and singing to her babies. Then she would yell out to us randomly, "I love you, goodnight!" Zach and I were giggling.

Then all was quiet about an hour into it, so we figured she crashed. But then like Horton Hears that Who, we heard the ever-so-faint voice. We grabbed the baby monitor out of our room so we could hear what she was saying. She was singing "Mary had a Little Lamb." But, she kept singing it differently like: MARY had a little lamb, then she would say Mary HAD a little lamb. And on and on, accenting the next word. We were laughing so hard. Zach went in there and asked her why she wasn't sleeping, and she said she was just singing to her babies. So he left the room, and it was silent again.

Around 10:30, we hear, "Mommy, I need a tissue." I went in there, and she had a bloody nose. She had been picking her nose again! That is why she was so quiet. Her nose bleed stopped pretty quickly, which is why I think her platelets should be good! I told her not to pick her nose because if it didn't slow fast enough we would have to go to the hospital. She said, "Like that one time, when I stuck a stick up my nose?" That girl has a memory of an elephant! She had stuck a stick up her nose when she was 2, and we had to take her to the ER because when we asked her what stick because nothing was visible, she said "Its still up there."

So finally, around 10:45, she fell asleep. I am about to wake her up in 20 minutes, and she is NOT going to be a happy camper. She prefers at least 12 hours of sleep at night, always has.

I'm also excited today because the weather is going to be GREAT for the next two days, and I hope she can get out and play! She is getting such cabin fever. I will say, however, she has learned to use the mouse on the computer wonderfully and can fully navigate PBSkids.org. She is on there most of the day and getting good at the puzzles. I feel guilty letting her sit in front of electronics all day (either the computer or her Leapster Explorer), but I've got to give the girl something to do that doesn't involve mommy and daddy at her side constantly. She would welcome a break from us; I know she would.

Well, I better get off this thing and get ready to head to Peoria... the early bird gets the worm there. First come, first serve! And I want to be done as soon as I can so Lucy can come home and play in the back yard! Yea!!And our water is getting done today too! Woo hoo!! Crystal clear water to bathe in tonight.....so excited!!

Day 85, Mar 21, 2011 7:58am
Really? It's been since Wednesday when I last updated? Things have been and always are, so crazy around here, that time just flies by.

Well, Lucy and I did clinic in Peoria Wednesday, and her numbers had dropped pretty low. Her ANC was only 220, so no going outside for her, :(and we had to go back on low bacteria diet. It's easy enough to make, but Zach and I are so sick of processed food! And when we got home from Peoria, they were still working on the water system. Took them all day. I think my uncle worked on it for like 8 hours, and after he left, Zach had a couple of hours of things to do, but... proud to say we now have clean water that Lucy can bathe in!! Woo hoo!!! She took the longest bubble bath on Thursday. The water wasn't orange or brown and the bubbles lasted the entire time!!

Wednesday night, the kids and I made a leprechaun trap while daddy finished the water system. They were a little excited and worried. Jack was worried our trap wasn't good enough and the leprechaun would get away, Lucy was worried the leprechaun would sneak in her bedroom at night and mess with her babies!! In the end, the leprechaun got away and left the kids chocolate gold coins. As happens every year, Jack coveted his treasure and ate the coins slowly and still has some; Lucy ate hers in one sitting!

Thursday, we asked my mom to watch the kids for a few hours so we could run errands and, frankly, just get out of the house at the same time. We took that opportunity to look at new minivans. Our Vue was starting to have so many problems, and we were sinking tons of money into it. Plus, with all the trips we will be taking for the next 2.5 years, we need all the room we can get. Let me tell you, I was definitely a little bummed about ownership of a minivan; I wanted a Mini Cooper! But, we did end up finding a used Town and Country that was exactly what we were looking for, had low miles, and an awfully low price. We jumped at it and drove home in our new vehicle. Didn't quite plan on taking it home that day, but we had been looking for a few weeks, and the one we first laid eyes on and wanted was sold the day before we made our offer, so we weren't going to make that mistake again. So the Webers now have a swagger wagon!! Lol!

When we brought it home, the kids were thrilled. Lucy sat in the 2nd row seating and Jack in the third. So no fighting! Genius!! And the DVD system was worth its weight in gold. Not to mention, it runs and is safe, unlike the condition of where our other vehicle was heading.

Friday was a full day at home to clean, and it seems like I cleaned the same thing over and over and, by the end of the day, the house was still wrecked! I do not know how stay-at-home moms do it. It's probably the most frustrating thing for me. I don't have a sense of accomplishment at home because everything is ongoing and never finished for more than a few hours. I'm a better office mom. That I have learned and now I have to adjust to this change which could be one of the hardest. It doesn't help that we are cooped up inside since Lucy's numbers were low.

Saturday, I took Jack to a friend's b-day party (his first non-family party -- what a huge milestone for both of us). I got to drop my baby off and leave. I was nervous; he didn't care! Lol! I then went and had lunch all by myself, and it was pure bliss. To sit and eat with nobody nagging me. I got to people watch and collect my thoughts. It was wonderful.

Saturday night, Zach and I were going to go out and see a local band for a few hours while my mom watched the kids. We were so excited and got all ready. We stopped for dinner first, then anxiety hit me like a ton of bricks. For some reason, I just wanted to go home. I knew Zach didn't, so I felt bad when we pulled in the drive and he didn't want to go in the house. Then I lost it.

We sat out in the van while I cried. I finally cried. I cried about how unfair this is, I cried about how I want our old life back, I cried about how scared I was. And I just sort of lost it. Really, the first time I ever used the phrase "this isn't fair." I've tried to avoid it up to now, knowing that it's so cliché and that nothing is ever really "fair," so why dwell on it. But that is exactly how I felt at that moment, and it, quite frankly, sucked. I just wanted to crawl into bed and come out when this is all over.

We went inside and Zach took my mom home while I tucked the kids into bed. Then a friend of mine came over and that helped a lot. The three of us stayed up pretty late just laughing about what sucks with cancer.

Now I'm caught up to yesterday... told you a lot happened! Yesterday, we took Lucy to get her blood count to see if we were good to head to Memphis, and her numbers are high, so we started packing. Jack's on Spring Break, so he's coming with us this time. We thought we'd get on the road yesterday, stop halfway, and finish the trip this morning. That would give us an extra day in Memphis before high dose chemo and while Lucy's numbers are still high enough that we could take the kids to the zoo. Didn't want jack to say he spent his spring break at a cancer hospital watching his sister get chemo and that was it.

So we packed the swagger wagon (which is huge!!), loaded up, and headed out around 6 pm. Plans were to drive halfway and stop for the night. We stopped about 90 minutes into the trip to let the kids stretch, and Lucy said, "Where's White?" OMG!! We had left White at home!!!!

So, I'm typing this from home! We turned around, came back home, and just slept here. A girl should be able to have her favorite baby while getting high dose chemo. So today, we will head out and do the whole trip in one shot! Wish us luck!

Day 87, Mar 23, 2011 7:43pm
Lucy's procedure went well today. They added a mix of Benadryl to the cocktail, and she slept longer, didn't wake up angry, and no vomiting! Yea!! No dizziness either. We may have found our perfect cocktail!

She is now inpatient, getting her high dose methotrexate. Our very last one, which will also mark the end of our 2nd phase of treatment. On to round 3, which is 120 weeks long!

Jack got to come to Memphis with us, so he and I are at the RMH while daddy stays with Lubelle. He was at the hospital from 8:30 this morning till about 5:30, and he was ready to leave! And having both kids in a small room... we were ready to bust him outta there! At least yesterday, we got to spend the whole morning at the zoo. Gives him something to talk about for his Spring Break.

The kids loved the zoo. Daddy and I would have been just as happy watching the monkeys all day (hilarious), but Jacks mission was to see every single animal! And we almost did. We stayed away from the reptile exhibit and night animals because we were told the breathing environment wasn't the best for Lucy and that there were cockroaches in one of them. Yuck! Beyond that, we hit them all.

The evening before, we took the trolley through Memphis and then a horse-drawn carriage that looked just like Cinderella's. Lucy kept saying she was a princess. ;) We also ate downtown at Huey's. Lucy got up, in Lucy fashion, and danced in the middle of the restaurant. She wore a dress that night and kept saying, "I want everybody to see how gorgeous I am." No problems with self-esteem in this one! ;)

We got a 2:15 start on the chemo, so hopefully she will clear it enough to come back to RMH late afternoon on fluids; then we can go home-home Friday if all is good. We won't have to come back to Memphis for 6 weeks, and when we do, it will be day visits so one parent will be flying with her. Can't say I'm gonna miss the drive. ;) We get our roadmap for our next phase at the end of the week and will do weekly visits to Peoria.

Again, I am rushing this, and we JUST started our high dose! Ha! Ok, ok. One day at a time. Let's hope Lucy clears her Methotrexate tonight so we can sleep as a family tomorrow.

CHAPTER 7
OUR BUMPY START INTO MAINTENANCE

Day 90, Mar 26, 2011 7:25pm

Well, we are home-home!! And it has been nice all day. We pretty much didn't do a darn thing! Ha! I did go grocery shopping, since our milk and eggs had expired, and we put clothes away, but other than that, nothing.

The kids have been playing and fighting all day, so that's nice. Yesterday, we ended up driving all the way home. The place we normally stop didn't have one single room available since there was some sort of track tournament going on. If we stopped at the next town that had available rooms, we would have been 2 hours from home, so we forged on.

Lucy threw up on the way home and is having a rough time with the 6 MP chemo she takes. Unfortunately, this is the one she will be taking for the next 2 years, too. Since she is all done with Phase 2 and her Methotrexate, they upped her dose to a full dose, and it really makes her sick. Thank goodness for Ucky Chucky barf bags (yes, that is the name of the bag!). We now carry them in our van at all times. They work awesome, but need some sort of technology that blocks the smell a little better!

Lucy seems to be doing ok today as long as we keep giving her Zofran around the clock and, if she is sick when she's not due for a dose, we have Benadryl that they gave us for nausea too. It works great, but makes her crash. We also know her numbers will crash by tomorrow or Monday. Her ANC had already dropped from 2600 to 2000 in one day, so we expect her to be neutropenic by Wednesday. Then we go to clinic on Friday. Next week is our week "off" from office visits, so Friday we will hopefully get our roadmap for how the rest of our treatment will go. I am anxious to see what kinds of chemo she gets and when she gets them. Also anxious to see her schedule of dex (steroid). NOT looking forward to that one! They say the fits on dex are far worse than Prednisone. Awesome.

I'm glad this time we actually get to unpack our bags. We are home for 6 weeks, which will give us enough time to actually get a routine going, pull in paychecks, and take Lucy to clinic. It should be less stressful and hopefully, we will get some sort of normalcy around here. As normal as it can be anyhow.

We also have to make some doctor appointments for Zach and me. We both have some health stuff that we have put on hold, and it really needs to be taken care of. Poor Zach and his tooth! LOL! And I have to find time to make a trip to Mayo. I'm due for my yearly visit for my Hashimato's disease, and the doc won't refill my script if I don't go see him. UGH. That's an 8 hour drive, and this time I'll have to do it by myself since we can't leave Lucy. And of course, Jack definitely needs to be able to talk to somebody. So Monday, I'll call to get him into a counselor. He definitely is having some issues, but heck, we all are.

Cancer really screws with everybody in the family, mentally. Lucy was crying yesterday and wanting something (I don't even remember what it was), and Jack looked at her and said "People give you what you want when you cry because they feel bad for you because you have cancer; heck, even I feel bad for you, Lucy." I didn't quite know what to say. He hit the nail on the head. So, he is observing and taking all this in and doesn't have anybody to talk to about it. I try, but he is worried about making me stressed out, so he doesn't want to talk about it. So, that is my #1 priority this week.

Taco is home! Sure did miss that little booger. He's more cuddly than normal, must realize he really does love us after all. :) Well, it's about that time to get the kids settled in for bed; then I am sitting my butt on the couch all night.

Day 96, Apr 1, 2011 5:09am
Wow, I can honestly say I haven't been up this early for quite a while. Usually, 6 is my sweet spot. For some reason, I was tossing and turning last night, which I guess isn't too abnormal; I do that most nights, but usually, I know why, and last night I'm not sure. We do have clinic today, so it could be nerves. We will find out

Lucy's numbers, and we will get a roadmap on the rest of her treatment (hopefully). Zach and I are both anxious to see what types of chemos and meds she gets during the next 120 weeks and how much and when. This will be the closest to being able to plan that we have had in a long time. Funny thing is that I used to have the schedules, calendars, and plan in advance, and Zach used to be the laid back go-with-the-flow type of guy. Last night, he said, "Man, I need to have a plan and see what her roadmap is. It's driving me crazy." I thought it was ironic since I think he is more anxious than I am! Funny how this has changed each of us.

The last week has been great at home, but exhausting. Yesterday and Wednesday were almost as "normal" as you can get. I worked both days, one from home and one from the office, and then had all kinds of things to do at home. So I actually was able to hit the pillow and sleep.

That hasn't been the case in the past weeks. Usually, I haven't slept much at all. Night time is still the worst, even at home. It's when you have to time to think, and sometimes, you don't like all the things running through your brain. Zach is the same way. We are dead-tired, but when we lay down, we just stare at the ceiling. So, being able to get a routine going is seeming to help a bit. We also had some good family time this week.

Monday we had a Nerf gun war! It was awesome for about 45 minutes, then out of nowhere, Lucy got a bloody nose. She was just standing there, too! It's things like that that catapult you back to reality.

Tuesday was my birthday, so we had a little mermaid party! LOL! The kids decorated balloons with stickers, and we had cake and ice cream. Then, Lucy gave me a purse! She insisted daddy buy me one for my birthday. I got the BEST 3-year-old purse. :) I will definitely be sporting that one this weekend.

Lucy is also back to normal in a lot of ways, which can be scary. That little girl has my clumsy gene. This week, she has managed to get a black eye, pull a chair down over her head, run into her bed post SEVERAL times, and run into a wall or two! LOL! Good thing her platelets are high. But, the new, added stress of clumsiness plus cancer is definitely something I did not anticipate! She is also a very bored little girl.

Lucy is social by nature, so being cooped up at home with us has made her a grouchy bug. We try to keep her busy by playing school, games, and then letting her do activities, but she is happiest when Jack is home, even if they do fight almost the entire time. She is also dying to go outside. I hope her numbers are ok today and on the rise, so we can let her play in the nice weather we are supposed to get next week.

Last night, Jack was outside, and she stood by the window giving me a play-by-play of what he was doing. It was so sad. We did ask our nurse, Martha May, about going outside and what the rules were, and she said as long as she isn't playing in the dirt, she will be fine. Well, this is Lucy we are talking about. And I don't know what else she would be doing out there! Ha! She is a "get dirty" type of girl, and sitting on the sidelines is not her cup of tea. So, I hope for an ANC of more than 500 today.

We did get Jack into see a counselor, and I don't know if it helped him any, but it sure did help me! The guilt I have built up from him being left behind the past couple of months was really getting to me. The counselor talked to us and helped to let us see that what we did was a "have to do" type of situation and, that if there is any damage done to his spirit, it's not irreversible. He helped to validate some of our feelings and fears, and Jack talked to him about the things he was feeling, so I think we are on the right track there, and I feel a ton better about it. It's a start.

He had said we need to do some things for ourselves as well and to make sure that is a priority. He said it even has to be a priority over the children right now. He said, "How can you expect to take care of them if you can't take care of yourselves?" It's weird, but it was nice for someone to give us "permission" to be selfish. I decided to take care of myself by signing up for Weight Watchers and working on that first, and it's been nice counting points. It's the one thing that I have absolute control over in a day. Odd that being on a diet would be a comfort! Ha! We are also going to go sign up for the gym. What better way to relieve stress and quite frankly, just get out of the house? Living here, taking care of Lucy here, working from here... we need separation. So, we are going to take turns going there for an hour every other day or so. Plus, what a great stress reliever. We have also made more time for us to go out on dates.

Now, they aren't your go-to-a-movie date! Like last night, we had my mom watch the kids while we went and shopped for new pillows. And it was actually a lot of fun and a nice change. I can honestly say that this has brought Zach and I closer. They say something like this can break a marriage and family up. And in the beginning, we would often talk about that. We would say, "I wonder what this is going to do to us." We were very aware, and at times, it was uncertain, because we would pick at each other when we were feeling bad. But now, after going through what we have in the last 3 months, I think we are a stronger couple, and definitely getting back to being best friends like we were when we first met. Hopefully that continues.

Well, I know I did a lot of rambling, I really needed that! Whew! I will update about her numbers and roadmap as soon as I can. Thank you for the continued support; it means the world to us to know we have a cheering section behind us. And if Lucy realized all the people who were following her, she would be tickled pink. She is definitely the type of personality who likes to be seen. :) Heck, when we go out she always asks, "Think people are looking at how beautiful I am?" LOL! Or she wants everybody to see when she is wearing a Beatles shirt! She's a nut.

Day 96, Apr 1, 2011 5:40pm
Well we have a 620 for an ANC count. So we are higher than the 500 cut-off for low bacteria diet and heading outside. But, they aren't sure if her numbers are going up or down, which could mean in two days they could be below the cutoff point. So, we will let her play outside tomorrow and then wait until clinic on Tuesday to see how they are doing and treat her as nuetropenic

from Sunday on.

We got our "schedule" for the next 6 weeks. Next Tuesday marks day one of our next phase of treatment. So we are officially in Continuation or Maintenance! Woo hoo! 120 week countdown to start!

Next week, we get to start steroids. Joy. She's on Dex for 5 days, then off for two weeks, then on again for 5 days. She also will get Vincristine again and small doses of Methotrexate. No spinals for the next 6 weeks, and doc said her numbers will more than likely be good through the next 6 weeks! So yay!! And of course she continues on the oral 6mp chemo every night.
At least we have a calendar and some idea of what to expect. Now to enjoy our weekend before the evil Lucy on steroids joins us next week!! Lol!

Day 103, Apr 8, 2011 10:19am
Well, It's been awhile since I updated, mainly because we have been busy here at the Weber household. One little girl on Dex (steroids) = lots of time preparing food for her! Although I will say, she is not as bad on this than she was on Prednisone, but then again we are only on day 4. She only takes it for 5 days, then she's off for two weeks, and then she takes it again for 5 days. The Dex doesn't seem to make her nearly as angry as the Prednisone, but more emotional. Poor thing doesn't know if she is coming or going. And the lost look in her eyes when she has a Dex meltdown is the saddest thing I have ever seen.

She also got an IV drip of Vincristine Tuesday and that is starting to affect her as well. She is starting to get the neuropathy pain that is associated with that. We are waiting on our Gabenpenton to arrive to help treat that. We were supposed to have it and give it to her two days prior to Vincristine (Peoria neglected to tell us this; Memphis called to let us know, and they also ordered it for us). So we like Peoria, but they are not Memphis.

Memphis is much more organized, timely, and more conservative with their approach to how to treat Lucy. We like being as cautious as possible. Peoria is more lax about everything. I'm sure we will get used to that, but for now, we are missing Memphis at times.

She did get to play outside 2 times this week because her numbers were good enough, but now we are certain they have crashed after upping her dose of the nightly chemo and adding the Vincristine in there, so its inside for Lucy until Tuesday clinic to check her numbers. Next Tuesday, she gets another low dose Methotrexate. Basically, it looks like our schedule is one week of Vincristine and Dex, and two weeks of Methotrexate, and repeat. And, of course, the nightly chemo is what she is on for the next 2.5 years.

We are trying to find our normal routine here at the house with Zach and I both working from home and taking care of Lucy and taking turns taking her to clinic. We may have found a good routine this week. We also made sure we joined a gym so that we can get out of the house and release some stress! It was funny because it was doctor's orders to exercise. Not that we didn't need to do that anyhow, just funny how much exercise helps. I think the thing we are fighting the most is cabin fever. We can leave sometimes, but then every time you go out, you risk coming in contact with somebody that is sick or getting sick, and I don't want to bring that home to Lucy. I wash my hands and use sanitizer a lot, but it's not fool-proof. I just want to get through the end of the summer and her intense chemo sessions and not have any delays. We did get our calendar for our Reinduction phase. We have to be in Memphis on May 17th, and will be there for at least a month, perhaps 5 weeks.

We aren't certain how we are going to do it, since Jack is in the last two weeks of school at that time. Plus, we already know how he did in Memphis for just 4 days... he won't make it for a long period of time. We may just have one parent stay home with Jack, do a "visit" to Memphis when school is over, and then come back home. We may even get lucky, and Dr. Pui may let us do some of it back at home, although we aren't sure how we feel about that.

We would love to be home, but with her numbers crashing all the way to zero during this period, we would rather be in Memphis. They would give her preventive antibiotics there; they won't in Peoria. There, we would be 5 minutes away from a hospital if she got a fever (which is common during intense chemo sessions). We are an hour from Peoria, and an hour is a long time in our situation. So that is still not decided.

Overall, besides getting super-tired and not being able to get quality sleep (steroids), Lucy is doing well. She is bored, so we are trying to come up with new fun things to do. I think she is sick of Zach and me!! LOL!

And her hair is growing back very nicely! It's dark, dark black, like it was when she was a baby. Too bad it will fall out again during our Reinduction. Well, I think steroid girl wants yet another breakfast... going on #4 now. ;)

Day 106, Apr 11, 2011 7:07am
Yesterday was not a great day here at the Weber household. Lucy experienced her first real pain since this venture started. Well, besides the first week... She is having lower back pain really bad, which I am assuming is from the Vincristine. It causes nerve pain, so it can pretty much touch any part of your body. It usually focuses on legs and jaw pain, but Lucy was crying and screaming yesterday that her back hurt. It was horrible. We have Codeine to give her, but it only lasts about 4 hours.

We are waiting for her Gabapenton to arrive; it was supposed to be here Saturday via Fed Ex. Hope it's not sitting in a warehouse or on some guy's truck or we won't be able to take it. It's a perishable med that has to be refrigerated.

Yesterday was tough on Zach and me. To watch your child go through so much pain and agony and for there to be nothing you can do for it. Then Zach was cleaning out a laundry basket and as he dumped it out, all of Lucy's hair clips fell out. He pretty much lost it at that point. It just reminded us what has happened, the severity, and that we have such a long journey to go through. You try to be "normal," and, in fact, you're far from it.

And Lucy never complains, so if she is complaining and crying and screaming, it has to be bad. I think her finally being off Dex is making it worse. The steroid boosts the pain meds and anything else in her body, so the pain was probably masked a lot from it. So now she's off that, which also comes with the side effect of crashing. Dex is like drinking 8 cups of coffee 3 times a day, and then all of a sudden you stop. I hope she sleeps a lot the next few days.

Today, I hope for a better day, and I hope her clinic visit goes well tomorrow. She gets a low dose of Methotrexate. We know how her body reacts to that, so we are hoping the Vincristine will be out of her system in the next day or two.

Yesterday was a beautiful day in central Illinois, and Lucy tried to go outside at one point, but said she just wanted to "relax" on the porch. I think that was the most depressing. She should have been running around the yard, and she was sitting. I hate that she's missing out on her childhood. She's 3, and the wonderment and imagination of a 3-year-old is grand. I don't want her to spend it inside on the couch.

It makes me angry. I know it's necessary, and that when we are done with these next 3 years, it will have been so worth it. I read an article about a 25-year-old from Bloomington who had ALL when he was 8, and has been cancer free since he was 11 (they calculate the start as when you are finished with treatment); it was a great story and I hope that when Lucy is 25, we will be saying she has been cancer free for 19 years.

Day 109, Apr 14, 2011 10:27am
We have had much better days yesterday and, so far, this morning. Lucy played outside all of yesterday. She also got a visit from her best friend, Cole, and he brought her pictures of all her friends at her old daycare. She has carried the pictures around ever since. She misses seeing her friends and gets upset that she won't be able to go back.

We have had no pain the past two days, and since her numbers were high, she gets to be "normal". It's awesome. We grilled out for dinner and ate on the deck. Lucy loves to eat outside. We were told to expect her numbers to fall quite a bit by next Tuesday since she is off the Dex, so we are enjoying this week to the fullest. Tomorrow is Jack's school carnival, and I think we are going to let her go. We go back and forth, but may as well let her enjoy these days! And, if we get paranoid about sick kids, we can always make her wear a mask.

Thanks for the nice comments and support. It means the world to Zach and me, especially when we were having a rough time over the weekend

Day 110, Apr 15, 2011 7:29am
So I mentioned that Lucy got pictures of all her friends at her old daycare? She hasn't put them down! Lol! Poor thing misses them so much! She has phone conversations with them on her pretend phone. Last night, she went to sleep with her pictures and was sticking her hand out her door trying to get some light so she could see them better! It was funny and sweet and sad all at the same time. I so wish she could go back to daycare to play with them.

Tonight is Jack's school carnival and we made the decision to let her go. I hope we made the right decision. She needs out of this house just as much as the rest of us! I think I'm more excited than Jack! Lol! I keep saying "Know what tonight is?" and he keeps saying, "Mom!! I know!!!" Ha!

Yesterday, she was a bit tired all day from playing outside so much the day before. Since it's going to rain today, she will get lots of rest and hopefully be geared up for tonight. I'll try to post pictures but Caringbridge is finicky about pictures, so I may have to open a public Google album. I'll work on that over the weekend.

Day 113, Apr 17, 2011 8:36am
Well, we made the most of our week of "good numbers". If it was

sunny, Lucy was outside. We even made it to Jack's school carnival on Friday. We were nervous about taking her around other kids, but felt comfortable enough to put her in a mask and let her play some games. We hung out in the bingo room and dance room for some time because those were the rooms with fewest people. She had so much fun. She still talks about getting out of the house!

This week her numbers should be going down, not nuetropenic, but probably below 1000 for ANC. Tuesday clinic is another "easy" chemo. Methotrexate, but a super low dose. So numbers will probably be lower, but looks like rain most of the week, so we will hang inside anyhow.

This is the first year we aren't having family over to our house for Easter. It is a little sad to me because I love doing the Easter egg hunt for all the cousins, but we decided with all that entails, we didn't need the added stress. Next year, it's on, and I'll do the biggest and best egg hunt ever! Lol!

Zach is putting together a play set for the kids in the back yard, and it's coming along nicely. That will give Lucy something to do while we are home this summer. He has worked on it for a week now, and I think it's half done! Ha! It's a little bigger than we thought. Oops! Hopefully, it'll be a good place for her to hang and use her imagination while Jack is doing his activities.

I also inquired to some places about getting her a tutor to come in two times a week. Since she will be missing preschool, we thought we should at least get somebody in here to make sure she will be ready for kindergarten when it's time. We work with her, but she gets tired of boring parents! I think she would relish in the idea of a "teacher" coming each week. Make her feel important, and give us a break! Even if it's only an hour at a time.

Since we have been home, she has been on me like glue. Always in her line of sight! Ha! I try to look at that as a positive out of this whole ordeal. I would never have gotten this time with her otherwise. And for that I'm grateful.

Day 116, Apr 20, 2011 7:43am
Yesterday wasn't too bad. Lucy went to clinic and got sick after her push of Methotrexate, but they gave her Zofran through her IV so it was all good. The only other eventful thing was her going around and teaching other kids how to sing "SpongeBob poopy pants." Give me strength! I would like to apologize to anybody else who was at clinic if your child learned a new song!!

My mom came over last night so Zach and I go could out to dinner. It was a much needed break. Being cooped up in the house sure can take a toll on your mood. We went to the Caboose here in town and then headed to Toys r Us to top off the kids' Easter baskets. I think we had more fun browsing the store than anything! Then, on the way out, you know the machines that have the toys and gum in them for 50 cents? Well, Zach saw a mustache machine and couldn't pass it up! So we bought fake mustaches and wore them home. I'm sure the people there thought we were nuts! I was laughing so hard. It's the little things. We wore them home and Lucy and Jack just laughed and giggled so hard.

I would also like to think our wonderful fans and supporters at The Castle Theatre here in Bloomington. They are having a band, American English, who are a Beatles cover band, on Friday night, and they have arranged some pretty special events for Lucy. I'm so excited!! We haven't told her yet, as we have to make sure her ANC is above 1000 so we can go. So we get it checked Friday morning. I hope she has good numbers. She will get to meet the band, have a song sung to her, "Lucy in the Sky with Diamonds," and dance all night to their songs! They arranged our own seating area, which is awesome so she's not in the middle of people. They are amazing... so a big shout out to The Castle!! Go support your local businesses. ;)

I had a really rough night last night. Not sure why, but the tears were flowing until about 1 am. Sometimes I think I bottle up everything, and eventually it needs to be released. Sometimes I'm just more scared than other times. Scared because I start reading other people's Caringbridge sites, and they start out similar to our experience and then something goes horribly wrong. I know I need to stop reading these; I'm obviously not ready yet. But, sometimes I need to hear that the feelings others are having are the same as mine; it's a small bit of comfort. So last night was rough for me, but today seems better already.

Day 118, Apr 22, 2011 6:48am
I was talking to Zach last night, and I think I figured out why I haven't been sleeping and have more anxiety this week than normal. Easter is coming, and I'm having a hard time with holidays. The last holiday, x-mas, was when Lucy was diagnosed. So, I seem to be associating all things bad with the big holidays. He is the same way. He said, "Let's not make a big deal out of it and cook a big meal." So we aren't! Instead, we are doing brunch at Swingers Grille here in town. They have a fresh waffle and omelet bar, so we are comfortable taking Lucy and having her meal made fresh!

They'll still get their Easter baskets and egg hunt (by looks of it, it'll be inside), but that's it! Lol! I feel a little better now about it. Strange, I know, but doing something out of the ordinary gives me a little comfort. Man, if I have this much anxiety about Easter, I hate to see how our x-mases will be here on out!

This morning we are going to get Lucy's numbers checked to see where they stand. We have a very important show to go to tonight at The Castle Theatre! American English, a Beatles cover band, is playing and Lucy gets to meet the band!! We haven't told her yet since we don't know where her numbers will be. Doc said they should hold steady, but for our own peace of mind, we are welcome to get them checked. She has to wear a mask, but I'm fine with that. The Castle is also arranging our own seating, so that should help as well. Now to explain to her again it's not the real Beatles! Lol!

Lucy was also approved to make a wish for the Make a Wish Foundation!! Yea!! She hasn't officially told them what she wants yet, but she said she wants to eat with and meet the princesses, so I'll bet it'll be Disney. We won't go until she is all through with treatment, so we are looking at August of 2013. What a fabulous celebratory bash for her!! She will be done with chemo AND starting kindergarten the same month!!

It may seem a long ways away, but we are counting down our weeks. We are almost done with week 3 of 120!! Woo hoo! 117 to go! ;)

Day 121, Apr 25, 2011 8:20am
Well, I wrote an entry last night and apparently it didn't post. Grrr... We had a nice low-key Easter yesterday. It was kind of weird that we had no family over. The kids kept asking when we were doing the big egg hunt since I normally do that and have all the cousins over. With Lucy's numbers hovering around the 500 mark, I'm certain she is nuetropenic, and we didn't want to risk having lots of people over in our small house. Wouldn't be fair to make Lucy wear a mask in her own house. And it's been raining so much and there is so much moss outside, that mold grows easily, so we did an egg hunt inside, and on a much smaller scale.

We have some serious behavior problems with Lucy. She is 3, so it's things within that realm, but a bit worse with her isolation. It was so bad yesterday, at one point, I put her in her room because I felt it was better for both of us if she were in there a while. A safe place. I was apparently mistaken. I heard a crash and then crying. Apparently, her lamp had knocked over (still haven't gotten the full story on what she was doing), and she burned the entire side of her cheek and nose!! With her numbers low, a burn is the last thing we need.

First, her body has no immune system to heal it quickly and then there's the risk of infection. All over a burn. I put some prescription topical antibiotic on it last night called Silversept as it had a small blister. This stuff has actual silver in it, and it must be a miracle drug! This morning it's nearly healed! Thank goodness!!!

Zach and I are tired. Emotionally tired. It's a 24/7 around the clock job with worry, frustration, and uncertainty. I can't wait to go back to work. And I mean work in the sense of getting out of the house. After her Reinduction 2, that will be a greater possibility. Zach was looking at our neighbors across the way yesterday eating at the picnic table and having an egg hunt, and said, "Look at that family being all normal." We can't wait to get back to that.

I did get a visit from my uncle and his family from Indiana yesterday, and that was nice. It was good to have somebody to talk to! Man, we were all over them like we hadn't spoken to anybody in years! Lol... talked their ears off!! And Lucy was thrilled to have somebody to play with besides us. Soon, we will get back to that. Soon.

Day 128, May 2, 2011 10:44am
Wow, it's been a while since an update. I have been keeping more current on Facebook and YouTube, as those are more user friendly from my phone. If you are on Facebook, "like" Team Lucy to get up-to-the-minute updates and pics.

Anyhow, we have had a better week with Lucy's Vincristine. We started the Gabapenton 2 days prior to the push and are still using it 3 times a day. She has been "achy," but no outright screaming pain, so that's awesome! She also did well through the Dex. Saturday was her last day, so she should be crashing from that today. Her appetite is still fierce.

This week marks 5 out of 120!! Slow and steady wins the race. I was reading somebody's Caringbridge, and they said they had to remind themselves daily that they are running a marathon, not a sprint. How often I forget that. It seems as if we do a lot of waiting these days. Waiting for chemo, waiting for her numbers check, waiting for her numbers to rise, waiting to go back to Memphis, and, quite frankly, waiting to go back to somewhat of a normal life. We feel very isolated. And I know we are overly cautious, and some parents take the risk and let the kids go out more often, but I always see that a lot of those kids have the most complications, too. We are a no-complication kind of family. We really just want to get through her Reinductions, the most intense chemo, and then we feel we can take a deep breath and loosen the reins a bit.

Zach and I are lonely. We haven't had a lot of visitors and don't go out too much. Lucy is stir crazy and craving attention from anybody except her parents! Ha! I hope with the weather getting warmer, we can venture outside more and hope friends will come over. Outside is better... less risk of harboring or creating a Petri dish.

Clinic is tomorrow. Only small dose of Methotrexate. Let's hope for no drama.

Day 135, May 9, 2011 9:41am
Ok, our countdown begins for when we leave for our next long stretch in Memphis. Really? Already? And how's come our to-do list didn't get tackled while we were home?? So now that just places a little more stress on our last week home.

Plans are to leave Sunday after Jack's baseball game and drive halfway down, stop for the evening, finish our trip Monday, and check in that afternoon. We already have Tuesday and Wednesday jam-packed with appointments and procedures.

So this week we will wrap up assignments from work, pack for a possible 4-week stay in Memphis, attend Jack's baseball activities, get Lucy as much play time outside as possible, Jack has to have fillings for 2 cavities, we have a day of clinic, I have 2 doc appointments, and line up some things that need to be done to the house while Lucy is gone. All these things and more, and yet I sit here and complain instead of taking action! Lol! Oh, and I did mention take care of a very needy 3-year-old?

I think when we have so much to get done, I choose to hide under the covers and take zero action. Hahaha, as sad as it sounds, I'm looking forward to next week with only one thing to focus on. I obviously don't look forward to my daughter getting chemo or being put through all she has to endure, but focusing on just her instead of juggling is nice sometimes.

Because as nice as it may sound to some people, being able to

2 Kids, A Taco, And Cancer

work from home and be with your child, it's exhausting, and filled with guilt. Guilt when you are doing one and know you need to do the other, and sometimes (actually a lot lately), Lucy has demanded more attention than normal. Zach and I tag team and are mentally exhausted. So I guess the first start to achieving what needs to be accomplished is making a to-do list. Then I'll let you know if I'm actually making progress on that list or hiding under my covers!!!

Day 137, May 11, 2011 9:40am
Yesterday was clinic and our last one for 4 weeks while we are in Memphis. We are having a small problem with Lucy's GI tract as there seems to be some blood originating somewhere. They said since her platelets are fine, it probably wasn't internal bleeding from another source, but rather from her stomach. The chemo is so harsh on her little body. So, we are waiting for her to poop so we can see if it has resolved itself. Yes, you read that right. Waiting for a poop. It's like a newborn again where you never thought you'd have to evaluate a poop or that such an act could be so important. I hope it's all clear and that we don't have to make a trip to Peoria and be placed inpatient. Of course, you ask her to poop for you, and she refuses.

I made my lists!! And after yesterday's events, that's as far as I got. Been working all morning, wrapping up some work assignments, and trying not to stress out too much over this bleeding thing. As soon as I know anything, I'll update folks on where we are at.

Day 139, May 13, 2011 7:29am
Well, Lucy's bleeding has seemed to revolve itself. We have had no new incidents, thank goodness, but now we don't know where it originated from. Oh well, chemo is so rough, it could have been anything.

On a more positive note, today Jack's school is doing a Walk for the Cure and selling lollipops for Lucy. All proceeds from lollipop sales go to St. Jude! She gets to participate in the walk and is excited!! We have friends and family coming to watch her walk and support her and Jack. If you have a free hour, come to

163

Washington Elementary in Bloomington around 10:40-ish to watch her and Jack do their laps!!! And buy some lollipops! ;)

Day 141, May 15, 2011 8:32am
Today's the day. The day we leave for Memphis -- for we don't know how long. 3 weeks is the protocol, but based on how she does and the Pui factor as we like to call it, it could be 3 days-5 weeks. We hear rumors that Pui lets you do Reinduction at home now; we aren't sure how we feel about that since she will have crashed counts and need blood and platelets so often, not to mention no immune system, but if Pui is comfortable with it, and they give us a home nurse, we will trust his judgment.

We woke up to some flamingos on our yard. Yep, read that right! It's a fundraiser for the American Cancer Society. Somebody paid to have our yard "flocked." The kids loved it and it actually makes our yard look pretty good!! Hmmmm, who shall we flock??

We also woke to a leak in our water system. Yikes!! Of course the day we leave, we realize how bad it is. Going to have to make some calls to get that taken care of while we are gone.

The kids are about to kill each other. I already tried the whole guilt trip that they should get along because they won't see each other... didn't work. Well I hear Zach doing dishes so I better go help him get things ready and packed up. Plans are to pull out of town around 4, stop around 8 and get a hotel, and arrive in Memphis tomorrow around 1. Appointments start early Tuesday morning and procedure is Wednesday.

Day 149, May 23, 2011 6:04pm
Wow, it's been an entire week since I wrote the last journal entry. Mainly because of two things:
1. I've been busy at home (I stayed home with Jack since we had our water issue and had to make sure it was taken care of)
2. I've not exactly had happy moments to sit and write.

It's been a week since I saw my Lubelle and Zach, and today, I had a breakdown. I just cried. Not sure exactly what started the crying, but after it started, all it took was little things to get the tears a-flowing. Mainly, I cried because I'm a very unhappy, angry person today. Lucy is feeling the effects of chemo pretty hard, and she doesn't understand what is going on with her body and keeps asking her daddy questions that he can't give her answers to except "it's from the medicine."

The irony in it all is that she wasn't this "sickly" before the chemo even though her little body was filled with cancer. We honestly didn't know by her attitude. She slept a little more, but she had always been our little sleeper, so we didn't think much of it.

Last Wednesday, she had an MRI of the brain just to track her brain's progress after receiving all these medications and see where she ends up when we are all done. Funny thing is I got my monthly "cancer" magazine and it talked about the horrible effects of chemo on the brain. UGH....NOT gonna read that issue any time soon! All of these poisons kill the cancer, but unfortunately take their toll on her little body as well. For right now, we just sign consent forms promising not to sue or forms that we understand that the side effects can be horrible, and while we are signing these forms, we have zero control. Funny huh? The signing of the forms is the only control we have, and we give that up as soon as the ink hits the paper. But what are our other options? Take the risk of stopping treatment and see if the cancer may or may not come back? NOT a risk I'm willing to take since if it does, or already has, come back, it will come back with a vengeance. And if I thought the stuff she was getting now is bad... the stuff she would have to get later would be 10 times worse. No thank you; I'll take my risks as it is.

So what kind of poisons is she getting this week? Well, Wednesday, besides the MRI, which she had to be put under sedation for and was throwing up for hours afterwards because they still can't seem to get her "cocktail" right for putting her out, she also got her spinal tap where they inject 3 different types of drugs: Methotrexate, AraC, and Hydrocortisone. Then after that was over (4 hours to be exact), she got a push into her port of Vincristine and then Peg (short for a really long name of chemo) was ran for while through an IV. After a 13.5 hour day she got to go back to the RMH with daddy, where she proceeded to throw up again all night.

The next two days were ok. She seemed to have a bit more energy and also started her Dex steroid, or the demon steroid, as many parents call it.

Today and yesterday, she is having a rough time. She doesn't understand why her emotions are all over the place and why she is eating everything but the kitchen sink. She even asked Zach why she was still hungry when she wasn't really hungry. She's so smart. Zach will text me and tell me we are having breakfast #1, then #2...and so on with each meal. There are at least two of each and snacks in between.

I miss her terribly. I got a flyer in the mail for the Dells, and it made me cry. This time last year we were taking our first real family vacation to the Dells. The kids LOVED it; we LOVED it (even though toting around a 4- and 2-year -old was work), and we were so looking forward to returning this summer. Fat chance now.

I feel bad for both of my children. I try to make things normal around here (new normal), and I really am trying to accept the hand we have been dealt, but I'm angry today. Angry over this hand, and not for me, but for my children. I feel like they already got the short end of the stick having us for parents (ha! that's a joke), but seriously, now they have to deal with this crap at such a young age. And I know, I know....it will make them stronger, and blah, blah, blah, blah....I don't care. I would have preferred something else make them stronger.

To make my pity party even better, I was reading my bracelet that has the cancer prayer on it on what cancer CANNOT do. And as I read them, I said, "Well, it did that, did that, did that, did that." I know I need to pull up my big girl panties, but lately they just keep falling down!! And I think the elastic is broke! I need something to hold them up, and I'm searching for that something, my duct tape of sorts, and I have yet to find it. I am still looking.....

Anyhow, not sure how many people still read this since I post a lot of things on Facebook now, but if you are either here or there or would like to be in both places, just search for Team Lucy on Facebook, and you can see photos and such on there.

On Sunday, Jack and I will take the train to Memphis, and Zach and I will switch Lucy duty. I can't wait to kiss up on my Dex girl, even if she does say I am bothering her, like she did on the phone tonight. Ha! She will get Vincristine this Wednesday (the chemo that makes her hurt), and then next Wednesday she gets Vincristine and goes back on Dex and Peg again. Then, after that, we just wait until her numbers come back up before we can come home. Some say it takes anywhere from 3 days to 3 weeks. The majority of folks we have spoken with (even though each child is different) say plan to stay for 2-3 more weeks! LOL! So that is what we are doing. I will stay for the remainder of the trip, and Zach and Jack will come home.

Day 151, May 25, 2011 7:16am
Well, didn't exactly start the morning off on the right foot today. I learned upon waking that a family we had lived with at RMH lost their child, Brayden, early this morning to the vile and stupid beast we call cancer. Brayden is 6.

That is quite possibly the hardest thing through this ordeal. You meet lots of good people, families, and children, and you deal with the death of children on a very regular basis. It's no longer the story you read in the news, or the statistics you see, it's very real. And while it's a small "statistic" when you're reading about childhood cancer from the outside, every child lost is a huge number when you are living inside the world of St.. Jude.

Excuse my language, but every time I hear of another child losing their battle, I curse. My favorite words are: son of a bitch and the mother of all dirty words. It gives me a sense of satisfaction to curse at this evil disease.

Let me end this note by telling you about Brayden. Brayden was 6 and a rough-and-tumble boy. He made me nervous when he got on a bike or scooter! Lol! He had NO fear!! Very energetic and rambunctious. His grandma and I talked quite a bit. His mom always asked about Lucy and called her "the baby." She'd say. "how's the baby doing today?" And she had a look of determination in her eyes when she talked about Brayden. A look all mothers at St. Jude have. She did anything and everything for her children. My thoughts are with their family today, and I hope they are surrounded by family, friends, and love in the coming days, months, and years as they try to find their peace with Brayden's death, if that is even possible.

Day 156, May 30, 2011 8:35am
After a long overnight train trip to Memphis, Jack and I made it safely. Lucy said she was so worried about us and she dreamt about her "brudder" all night. So sweet and right to be together again.

As I walked into RMH, that familiar smell hit and a sense of calming peace and comfort assisted it. And not to brag, but the weather is pretty awesome too. ;)

Lucy goes into the hospital this afternoon for blood work, tomorrow she has clinic to visit with Pui, and Wednesday she gets two chemos and starts back up on an 8-day round of the demon steroid. Will keep everybody posted how our visit goes and how soon we get to go home-home ;)

Day 157, May 31, 2011 8:55am
For those of you following Odie's journey, Odie passed away last night/early this morning. Lauri could use all the virtual hugs available.

Day 158, Jun 1, 2011 7:57am
Lucy is at the hospital bright and early and ready for her last day of Reinduction 1. Another milestone in our 2+ year journey. She has one chemo that runs over 2 hours, so as long as there is no reaction to it, we plan on heading out tomorrow. We did find out

from Dr. Pui that Reinduction 2 will be done mostly from home. Since Lucy is in the low risk category for reoccurrence, she doesn't get two of the harsher chemos that standard and high-risk children get. So we were excited to hear that!

Yesterday was a hard day for me to focus on anything but our friend, Lauri. She lost her son, Odie, to a rare liver cancer. Odie was diagnosed less than a year ago. I've said it before; it's one the hardest parts about living in a world where children have cancer. Then today, another wonderful mother will find out if they have to remove her son's eye or eyes due to cancer. I have butterflies for both of these wonderful ladies today. There is nothing that can be said or done to make their pain go away or even ease it for either of them. One is filled with grief and the other filled with worry. I've said it before, in this world, cancer is dinner conversation, death is a common event, but it never ever gets "normal." Its devastation still hits me hard.

Today, I ask that you think of the children who are enduring their chemo, radiation, surgeries, or just managing their time and pain. Today, I ask that you think of the mothers, fathers, and siblings, as this has an effect on an entire family. Today, I ask you think of the children who have earned, and will earn, their angel wings today, tomorrow, and even for the ones who earned them yesterday. Today, I ask you think of the mothers who have to lay their children to rest due to cancer. And most importantly, today, I ask that you hug your own children, family, friends and know that it's ok to be very thankful that you are not one of above mentioned. I would never wish this on any other family or child, and my hope is, that within time, fewer and fewer will have to endure this world of children and cancer.

Day 159, Jun 2, 2011 8:24am
For Odie from his mom:
> *My sweet boy's obituary.*
> *13-year-old Odie Mason Harris of Bossier city LA., born Oct 1,*
> *1997, found his sweet release from a year long struggle with cancer*
> *in his mother's arms on May 31, 2011. Odie's family invites all that*

loved and supported him during this long, hard year and throughout his life to join them as they celebrate his young life and the fact that he is now free of all suffering.

Odie was a student at Elm Grove Middle School, whose staff and students went above and beyond to make sure Odie, even in his absence, always knew he belonged and was thought of everyday. The Bossier Sherriff's Office was instrumental in making Odie's dream of one day becoming a Marine happen in Jan, 2011 when he was made an Honorary U.S. Marine. Odie studied tang so do for 3 1/2 years at Pak's Karate in Bossier where he earned his black belt in Dec 2007.

Services will be held at 11:00am on June 4, 2011 at the First Baptist Church of Bossier in the Faith Chapel. officiating will be Rev Alan Pittman of the Life Journey Church and Chaplain Matt Impson of Jordans Crossing. Following the service, Odie will be laid to rest at West Lake Cemetery in Doyline, LA. Visitation will be from 5pm to 8pm on Friday, June 3rd at the Rose-neath Funeral Home in Bossier City, LA. Pallbearers will be his big brother, Adam Harris, his big sister, Malorie Crosby, his brother–in–law and in heart, Billy Szura, his loyal-to-the-end best friend, Braden Frith, his dearest friend and soulmate, Bill Bradford, and his friend for life, Kristen Hammett. Step-brothers Blake and Colton Stanley will serve as honorary pallbearers and be there to offer any needed support for this special group of Odie's closest friends.

Taken way too young, Odie is survived by his mother and constant companion, Lauri Hooper Harris of Bossier City; his devoted and always present father and step-mom, Terry and Bridgette Harris of Elm Grove, LA; his constantly caring grandparents, Hoyt and Jane Hooper of Doyline, LA; his loving older siblings and best friends, Malorie Crosby, Gennifer and Billy Szura, and Adam Harris, all of Bossier City; his step-brothers, Blake Stanley of Bossier City and Colton Stanley of Doyline, LA; and his sweet little niece, Marissa (Monkey) Stanley; and countless other members of a whole big, beautiful family.

Odie is proceeded in death by his grandaddy and grandmother, Max and Carolyn Harris, his uncle Mike Harris, his uncle Lynn Hooper, his memaw and papaw Hooper, his mamaw and papa Gulledge, and so many other beautiful souls...heaven is full of them.

Day 160, Jun 3, 2011 7:25am

We are home!!! We slept in our own beds last night. Woo hoo!! Today, we just have to get Lucy's counts checked at the local hospital and then she goes back to clinic Tuesday. She also gets a break from chemo until Tuesday. She started Dex though, so that's kind of rough on her.

She will go to clinic for the next two weeks, then Memphis again the week after that (it will be a short trip, so we are going to fly), then she is home until Reinduction 2 starts July 24th. Dr. Pui said she won't have to stay long for that one either!! Yay!! For summer, there is no swimming in public pools (boo) and no rivers or lakes due to the bacteria they harbor. But she can do splash parks and kiddy pools or private pools as long as we know somebody didn't pee in them! Lol! Our nurse, Martha May, said to have as much fun as possible :) just don't go far from home. So, we will be spending a lot of time in the backyard with sprinklers and water guns. After RI2, we will feel a lot more comfortable. Our treatment will also be a little easier.

The thing about leukemia is the harsh initial year of treatment, the duration, since it's a 2.5 year treatment, and since they keep their counts so low, the risk of infection. But, since Lucy is in such a high percentage of cure (99%, to be exact, is what Pui told us), we will do whatever it takes, even if that means 5 years of treatment!!!

After staying at RMH and seeing children who have relapsed from leukemia, children who have recently passed away, and children who don't have such a good prognosis, it's probably one of the hardest things Zach and I have had to live through. There is a sense of relief and guilt all at the same time, along with fear.

Fear that Lucy could relapse or get a secondary cancer, which is always a possibility. A sense of relief she is in remission and a sense of guilt for the same reason, in comparison to some of the other children. I can't make the relief and guilt go away, but I've been reading articles about adults who had leukemia to help relieve the fear.

We don't get to see or talk to survivors because we aren't in that place yet, but from what I have been reading, there are thousands who have normal lives, and after 10 years of being leukemia free, their chance of cancer is no worse than that of any other person. They have children and families and their children don't get leukemia. So that is helping calm my fears for now. And for now that's ok.

Day 163, Jun 6, 2011 7:16am
The weekend was a bit rough, and the house is a mess! We still aren't all the way unpacked. We really have found little time to do much of anything but separate the children and calm and feed our steroid girl. It's definitely been a tag team effort!

Lucy picks fights with Jack and the poor guy is so nice to her. They basically fight every waking moment with an exception here and there, plus the Vincristine Lucy had Wednesday is starting to rear its ugly head. She's pretty down and out and in some pain. The meds help, but then you have the steroid that intensifies it all. Plus, she is so worn down, but the steroid makes her want to go 100 miles an hour, so she is very confused. We have a million house things to get done. Our water system that was leaking and the laundry room got "fixed," and then we discovered another problem with our softener. Ugh! So we had to turn the system off. So poor Lucy hasn't even had a bath. We saw a carpenter ant outside on our deck; we are hoping they are just outside and not inside. Ugh!! Gonna have to have that inspected. Did I mention we haven't unpacked and that our house is a mess?? Lol! Jack starts summer camp today! Woo hoo! Keeping these two apart is the plan for the summer; trying to keep Lucy busy, and possibly away from us as much as possible, is part of the plan too. We are going to have some peeps come and help her with school stuff and even a babysitter to keep her busy here and there. It will give her a break from us allow us to work a little easier, but we are still close by if something were to happen. I am so looking forward to after RI2! She will be able to go to preschool a couple days a week for a couple hours and back to ballet. My social butterfly really needs it!

Lucy goes to clinic tomorrow for her Methotrexate and starts her nightly chemo again tomorrow too. I imagine her numbers will crash, and it will take her body a week or two to become adjusted again. The only bad thing about that is that I think Jack is coming down with a cold! Ugh!! Wonderful summer cold!

Well, steroid girl is up and ready to eat!! Better go feed that girl! ;)

Day 165, Jun 8, 2011 7:11am
Yesterday was our "normal" clinic day. Lucy said she was so happy to go see her friends. She absolutely loves "Shelby," whose real name is Shelly!! Ha! She's the child/life who coordinates all the activities and makes sure the kids have things to do while waiting for their chemo and doc visits.

Lucy got a push of Methotrexate and starts on her nightly chemo again. Usually that drains her, but she was up this morning, asking for food, and wanting to wear a dress, so I hope that means she will want to be a little more active. She has pretty much just laid on the couch and tortured the dog since we have been home. Poor Taco! Ha! She treats him like one of her baby dolls. I think the Vincristine she got last Wednesday just really wore her down when combined with the Dex steroid. It usually takes 7-10 days for the pain from the Vincristine to ease up, and this morning is her last dose of Dex! Woo hoo!! So I hope she gets off that couch and wants to play outside today. It'll be a hot one, and she can't play in the water yet since she was accessed yesterday, so I may have to get creative.

We return to Memphis on June 22 and already have made flight arrangements. I'll be taking Lucy solo this trip. We will leave on the 21st and return on the 23rd. Flying will help for the shorter trips from now on.

The only thing that stinks is that she is going to be on an airplane with recycled air, and we have a layover in Atlanta since there aren't many places that fly directly to Memphis. This will be her first airplane ride, so I hope she is excited and does well.

Zach and I are back to balancing life once again. It's rough at times. Every time I went to turn on my laptop for work yesterday, Lucy needed something. She wanted nothing to do with me while I wasn't on it! Lol! So nap times, after she goes to bed, and any time we can distract her are work times. And when do we clean and get other house duties done? We don't. Lol! And heaven forbid I leave her line of sight. Like now, I'm out on the porch drinking coffee and trying to type this, and she's been out to check on me at least 5 times! She's just a social butterfly and needs interaction. I will be thrilled when Reinduction 2 is over and we can expose her to that little at a time.

Day 167, Jun 10, 2011 11:15am
Lucy seems to be having her first fever today. :(She and Zach are at our affiliate to see what the next plan of action is. It keeps hovering right around 100.4, and that is when St. Jude patients need to be seen. They are going to run blood cultures to ensure there is no bacteria growing anywhere and move on from there. We will know more after her blood tests come back. If she does go inpatient, it's usually a 48 hour minimum stay unless it's something worse. I'll keep folks posted.

Day 167, Jun 10, 2011 5:04pm
By the time Lucy got to Peoria, her temp was down to 98.8. They still checked her counts and did blood cultures. We will know tomorrow by noon if she is getting some sort of infection. Her numbers were good, so they gave her some antibiotics to be on the safe side and sent her home. Thank goodness! They said this could happen from time to time with chemo and coming off Dex, it can just hover for a while but not spike… but better safe than sorry.

Day 172, Jun 15, 2011 7:51am

We have had a busy last few days since I posted last. After Lucy and daddy got back from clinic on Friday, we felt comfortable enough knowing she was well to have our first overnight getaway without the kids! So Saturday, Jack went to his Aunt Tines and little Grandma came and stayed with Lucy. It was nice to get a night out and wake up not having to meet everybody's demands except our own. It was a big step for us and shows it's possible to do again. So our new normal is coming along slowly.

Then Monday, we went to the St. Jude golf fundraiser here in town. Lucy met with a few golfers. She loved getting out and getting some attention.

Yesterday our Make a Wish coordinators came to meet with the family, and Lucy said she wanted to go to Disney and eat lunch with the princesses.

She loved having them come over. We rarely get guests because we are a little overly cautious, so she talked their ears off and played with them until they left.

At one point, I looked over at Jack, who was picking up his puzzle pieces, and he was staring at Lucy and the two ladies, and he asked for help in picking up his puzzle. We were saying, "You got it out, you pick it up". Well, his chin and lip started quivering, and it occurred to me at that very moment, he didn't really want somebody to pick up the stupid puzzle, he wanted the same attention Lucy was being showered with.

My heart broke at that moment, and I got on the floor and picked up the puzzle with him. He looked at me with the saddest eyes and softly said, "Thank you, mommy."

I forget sometimes how much this affects him as well and what it must feel like. This has been something that has always haunted me, and I'm not sure how to handle it. We took him to a counselor, and I find that I spoil him a little more when I should not. I know Lucy has cancer and chemo and goes through a lot physically, but her spirit is strong. I would bet that, emotionally, this whole ordeal affects her very little; it will just make her more spunky. Jack on the other hand, I worry about.

He has been acting out because, I think, he is craving attention, any attention he can get, even negative. I think we need to focus more attention on him. I often hear the guilt many parents feel towards the siblings of cancer children. Sigh... always something to do and worry about in this house; I wish for one day, we would have no worries...

Day 174, Jun 17, 2011 5:44am
Well I wished for one day with nothing to worry about, and while it wasn't perfect (still a few things popped up), yesterday was probably as close to normal as we are gonna get! It was one of the those days where I realized we are so accustomed to our new normal, that for the first time in a long time, I felt like we are going to be "ok." We are definitely going to stumble from time to time, but having days like yesterday make me feel like we have found our pace in this marathon. We weren't running too fast or too slow. Our breathing was perfect to make the long haul. Now, I know not every day will be like that, and that we will probably quicken the pace or fall behind from time to time, but knowing we are able to feel balanced, even for one day, was nice.

I'm not sure how many are aware, but the Webers are going to be on TV! Yikes! We have been asked for Lucy to be featured in the telethon this year on August 6th. The cameraman is coming today to interview our family.

As long as one of the kids doesn't say poop or anything else, I think we should be ok. And, of course, we are also worried about the word vagina. We were the ones that decided we would teach our children anatomically correct terms; we just didn't think they would overuse that word! It's gotten much better as Lucy has gotten older, but she used to tell anybody that would listen that she had one and that it was private. Oh my! And that's the family they ask to be interviewed for TV!! Good thing it's not live and can be edited.

So yesterday, we were cleaning the house, cleaned the back porch off (finally a day with no rain or stifling heat), Lucy harassed the neighbor, Nicki, all morning. Big thank you to her for keeping Lucy entertained while we got our stuff done. We were able to finish our projects in one setting and even do work! It was a good feeling of accomplishment. After we got Jack from camp, we had a small bonfire and made hotdogs and s'mores for dinner, the kids played outside, and then we threw them in the bath.

It was almost normal. Actually to our new situation (yes, we've been living with cancer now for almost 7 months, but it's still all new), it was a normal day and much needed. The kids didn't overly fight, we accomplished a lot of our to-do lists, and the only dramatic thing was the damn dog! Ha! Our wiener dog, Taco, got into the s'mores and hotdogs!! He's fine, just ornery.

Yesterday was also the first day I realized how grown up my babies are getting. Lucy has been helping me with meals by setting the table, Jack is old enough to take care of himself, and I about fell over when they both put their clothes in the dirty laundry without being asked! So, they do listen to me!!

I hope we have more yesterdays in our tomorrows to come, even if they just pop up every now and then. It makes me realize that giving cancer zero power or thought really is possible, even if for a moment. Now I know next week won't be as easy, but that's how the cookie crumbles.

Lucy and I fly for the first time to Memphis. She is ready for her first plane ride! She has a spinal scheduled for Wednesday to receive some chemo, then we fly home Thursday. Hopefully, a short trip, though she never does well with sedation. And it will be on my own, but we have to get used to this! It's 2 more years in this marathon, and that's quite a distance to go, but for now, we found our pace, even if just for a short distance.

EPILOGUE

174 days. I am amazed that is how long our front line treatment lasted. As I was going back and reading, I couldn't believe we were only on day 15 or day 20, it seemed as if it was forever. Those were the toughest 174 days of my life, and I believe for my families' as well. The next 174 were tough, but we seemed to get something back. We had adjusted to our new normal so much, it became our "normal". When they sat us down and told us our lives were going to be different, and we would adjust to this new normal, I never believed it to be true. Yet, here I sit and look around me. Everything is familiar, comfortable, and as it should be. It took us time to get here, and you will see that in the second series, how we got to where we are today. As well as meet many different personality of Lucy.

ABOUT THE AUTHOR

Shawna Weber lives in Bloomington, Illinois with her husband and two children, and one wiener dog. She has become an advocate for Children's Cancer Awareness and spends a lot of her free time helping to raise money for St. Jude Children's Hospital.

Made in the USA
Lexington, KY
30 August 2012